THE MOON RITUALS

96 Rituals for Making Magic with Every Lunar
Phase and All Zodiac Signs

by Sara Walka

THE SISTERS ENCHANTED

For Jacob, Ryker, and Imogen.

Keep your eyes to the sky and remember that anything is possible.

"You don't have to understand life. You just have to live it."
-Matt Haig, The Midnight Library

CONTENTS

Claim your free resources!

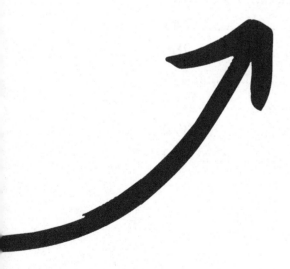

FOREWORD

Am I doing this right?

What if I mess it up?

I need to buy more magical items to make this work, look right, and be right.

......

When I began my magical, witchy adventure, my mind was filled with gremlins and negative thought spirals, insisting that everything had to be perfect. Altars needed to be pristine, with all the right rocks, herbs, and offerings. I felt I had to be perfectly aligned with each lunar phase to avoid squandering my intentions. And don't even get me started if someone touched ANY of my magical spaces!

There tends to be a vibe when you enter the witchy wilderness that if you aren't "witchy enough," then you aren't good enough to be here. Chronic perfectionism and overthinking run rampant, especially among women like me. And perhaps, like you.

That feeling—that you don't have it quite right—isn't an easy one to shake. It's human nature to want to get things right. But it's also in our nature to want to be present and connect with the higher versions of ourselves, or whatever we believe in. The pressure to create a personal practice that looks like it "should" instead of making one that fits YOU is real.

It wasn't until I released my need for perfection (or at least some of it) that I was able to develop rituals, create sacred space, and use my tools like tarot and astrology in a way that felt uniquely personal to me. When I leaned into myself as my most magical tool, with intention as my sidekick, it all started to feel a whole lot more like magic.

Instead of creating specific altar spaces that needed constant changing, I opted for drops of magic scattered throughout my home.

To most people, it looks like I'm just decorating.

But to the discerning magically inclined folks, they see bits of magic everywhere. There isn't a surface or nook in my home that couldn't be used for a ritual, big or small.

Even now, with the hands of tiny children that touch and move things, everything is still as magical as I intended it to be.

So, if you're finding yourself tangled in the web of perfectionism, remember this: Magic isn't about having the perfect setup or following every rule to a T. It's about the energy you bring, the intention you set, and the belief that your own essence is enough. Sprinkle magic in your own way, in your own time, and let your intuition guide you. Because the most powerful tool you have isn't on a shelf or in a book—it's within you.

Now, go out there and make some beautifully imperfect magic with the moon.

Stay weird, stay magic, and stay you.
Anna Tower
Co-Founder, The Sisters Enchanted

INTRODUCTION

The moon is a symbol of the cyclical nature of life, a guide for personal growth, and a powerful ally in ritual work. Understanding and working with the phases of the moon impacts our spiritual practices, emotional well-being, and personal development.

The moon's phases reflect the natural cycles of growth, fruition, and renewal that we observe in nature. By aligning our activities with these phases, we harmonize with the rhythms of the universe. This alignment fosters a connection with the natural world, enhancing our sense of belonging and grounding us in the present moment.

Each lunar cycle offers a blank canvas for coming back to intention. The New Moon, with its energy of beginnings, is the perfect time to plant the seeds of our intentions. As the moon waxes, we nurture these intentions, taking actionable steps towards their realization. The Full Moon, a time of culmination, shadow work, and reflection, allows us to assess our progress and celebrate our achievements. Finally, as the moon wanes, we release what no longer serves us, creating space for new growth.

The moon's phases are deeply intertwined with our emotional and spiritual states. Each phase resonates with specific energies – from the introspective New Moon to the expressive Full Moon. By attuning to these energies, we can embark on a journey of emotional and spiritual healing, using each phase as a guide to explore different aspects of our psyche and soul.

Rituals performed in sync with the moon's phases carry a unique potency. The waxing moon, with its building energy, is ideal for rituals of attraction and growth, while the waning moon supports banishing and release work. The Full Moon, with its intense energy, is perfect for powerful manifestation and healing rituals. Aligning our spiritual practices with the lunar cycle not only amplifies their effectiveness but also deepens our connection to the ritual itself.

Working with the moon phases is a journey of self-discovery. Each phase challenges us to grow in different ways – to be introspective, to take action, to express gratitude, and to let go. This cyclical process mirrors our own personal growth journey, encouraging continuous self-reflection and development.

The moon teaches us the value of patience and the importance of timing. Just as the moon takes time to complete its cycle, our intentions and goals require time to manifest. This understanding fosters patience and trust in the process, qualities essential for personal growth and spiritual development.

Working with the moon phases is not just a practice; it's a way of life. It offers a framework for growth, a tool for healing, and a path to deeper self-understanding. Whether you are new to moon rituals or a seasoned practitioner, the moon's ever-changing face is a constant reminder of the ebb and flow of life and the potential that lies within each of us to grow, transform, and shine.

Intention vs. Goal

Intention (n.): A thing intended; an aim or plan. (In medicine) The healing process of a wound.

Goal (n.): the object of a person's ambition or effort; an aim or desired result.

While the words "intention" and "goal" are synonyms, meaning they can be used interchangeably, we use the two words differently here at the Sisters Enchanted and you'll see this reflected throughout the book. We use the word "intention" to speak to how you want to feel. This is the emotional aspect of New Moon work. Go within, and essentially, set a goal (or intention as we call it) for how you want to feel. The word "goal", then, is used to set the actions you'll take to feel the way you want to feel. These actions are solar in nature and how you want to feel is lunar.

Here's an example for you:

Intention: I want to feel like I can breathe in my home.
Goal: Declutter the living room.

Intention: I want to feel awake and excited when I wake up.
Goal: No coffee after 2pm and go to sleep with no cell phone at 9:30pm.

The medicine of the moon is in its rhythm, so this lunar energy is used to set a feelings based intention that helps you heal an aspect of your inner world. Taking action to feel that way is done during your waking hours with the sun shining down and depends greatly on your confidence and what you do when the shadows appear. This, is solar in nature. Set your intention and set your goal each lunar cycle and create a life aligned with how you want to feel.

The Eight Phases

New Moon: A time of new beginnings and setting intentions. It's a period of darkness, both literally and metaphorically. This is when we go within to discover how we want to feel and what we'll do to feel that way.

Waxing Crescent: Here, we start to take small, actionable steps towards our intention and goal. It's a phase of building, nurturing, and gently pushing our dreams into motion.

First Quarter: This phase is about taking decisive action. It's a time to face challenges head-on and make significant progress towards our goals.

Waxing Gibbous: As we approach the full moon, our focus shifts to refining and trusting the process. It's about fine-tuning our actions and aligning them more closely with our intentions.

Full Moon: A time of culmination and reflection. We celebrate our progress, acknowledge the journey, and make any necessary adjustments to our path. And, we do shadow work.

Waning Gibbous (Disseminating Moon): This phase is about sharing our experiences and wisdom gained. It's a time to give back, either to ourselves or to others, and to practice gratitude.

Third Quarter: Here, we release what no longer serves us. It's a period of letting go, simplifying, and preparing for the renewal that the next new moon brings. We dream about what comes next.

Waning Crescent (Balsamic Moon): A time of rest, introspection, and preparation. We reflect on the past cycle and start to form our intention and goal for the new cycle ahead.

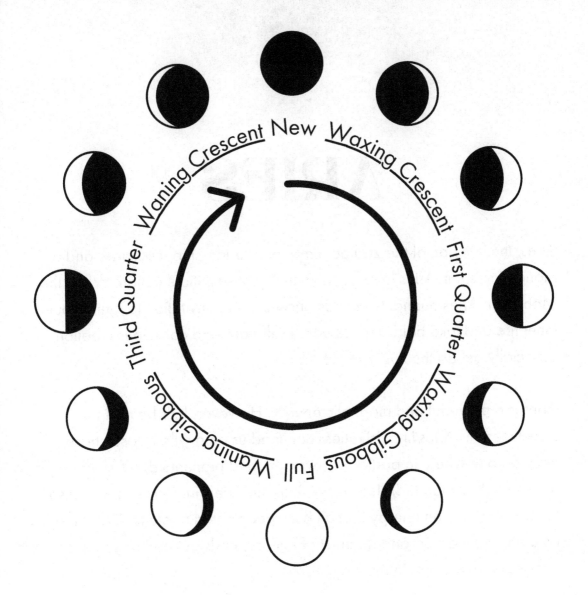

ARIES

Aries, the first sign of the zodiac, embodies leadership, courage, and a pioneering spirit. Aries loves to take charge and initiate action. When the Moon is in Aries during its various phases, it's an invitation to ignite your inner fire and take bold steps towards self-care and conscious creation, especially amidst the hustle of life.

Aries is a powerful and magnetic energy. However, let's be real – sometimes this Aries impulsiveness can lead us on a wild goose chase, ending up nowhere in particular (even the best pioneers don't always end up where they planned). Just as quick as the Aries fire ignites, it can also fizzle out. This is an energy that all busy people can relate to. What begins as a sudden idea or random burst of energy, ends as soon as someone needs you or life gets in the way.

In mythology Ares is the god of war and in the zodiac Aries is represented by the battering ram. We're invited to explore where we're going to war unnecessarily and where we need to make space to fight for what matters.

Aries Moon Toolkit

Here are some suggested tools for your Aries moon ritual kit. Keep in mind that everything is optional and the only true requirement is your energy, magic, and belief!

🌙 **Sun Sign Dates: March 21-April 19**

🌙 **Candle Color: Red**

🌙 **Oil or Essence: Ginger (for courage and initiative)**

🌙 **Herb: Basil (for strength and protection)**

🌙 **Spell Focus: Assertiveness and leadership**

🌙 **Element: Fire**   🌙 **Tarot: Wands**

🌙 **Crystal: Carnelian**

🌙 **Mythology: Ares or Mars, gods of war**

Aries In My Chart

Refer to your birth chart and look for Aries. It may be marked with this symbol: ♈

🌙 **House(s):**

🌙 **Planet(s):**

🌙 **Notes:**

Whenever the Moon is in Aries, it will highlight this part of your birth chart. You may notice heightened emotions in this area or shadow aspects of your life or energy coming to the surface.

ARIES
NEW MOON
Ignite Your Intention

ARIES NEW MOON
QUICKIE
For the busiest of magical bees.

Busy Witch Ritual:

Carve out a moment to yourself. Light a red candle, symbolizing Aries' fiery energy. Write down one bold, new intention and goal that excites you. Visualize it with passion and believe in its power. Blow out the candle.

Self-Care Tip:

Participate in a quick, energizing yoga session or a brisk walk to clear your mind and set your intention with clarity.

Affirmation:

I am one with the fiery strength and blazing spirit of Aries. Each day I courageously embrace new challenges and confidently pursue my passions. My actions are bold, my heart is brave, and my spirit is unyielding. I honor my inner warrior by nurturing my body, mind, and soul with self-care that empowers and rejuvenates me. I am fearless in the pursuit of what sets my soul on fire.

Aries New Moon Spell: Embrace the Warrior

Use this ritual at a New Moon in Aries to harness the pioneering and bold spirit of Aries for courage, initiative, and self-empowerment.

You Need:
- Red Candle
- A piece of paper and a pen
- A small piece of Carnelian or Red Jasper (stones of courage and vitality)
- A sprig of rosemary (for remembrance and protection)
- A small bowl of water

To Begin:
- Create your sacred space by finding a quiet place where you can be undisturbed. Cleanse the area with sound or incense smoke, inviting positive energy and dispelling any negativity.
- Light the red candle, focusing on its flame. Visualize the fiery energy of Aries filling the space, inspiring courage and bold action.

Set Your Intention:
- On the piece of paper, write down the qualities you wish to embody during this lunar cycle – such as courage, assertiveness, or the motivation to take action. Be bold and clear with your intention and goal.

To Begin:

- Hold the carnelian or red jasper in your hand, close to the candle's flame (but not too close). Imagine the stone absorbing the fiery energy, empowering it with the courage and initiative of Aries.

The Ritual:

- Pass the rosemary sprig over the candle flame (carefully) and then around your head, symbolizing protection and inner clarity. Place it beside the candle.
- State the following or something similar, "With the fire of Aries' bold light, I claim my power, my will, my might. As this new moon rises, so do my dreams. Fueled by courage, in my heart, it gleams."
- Dip your fingers in the bowl of water and touch your forehead, heart, and then the paper you wrote on. This act balances the fiery energy with emotional clarity and calm, nurturing energy.
- State the following or something similar, "As Aries leads with fearless tread, my spell is cast, my spirit fed. By the moon's new cycle, my intention set, in strength and peace, my path is met."
- Extinguish the candle. Do not blow out the candle; instead, snuff it out to preserve the energy.
- Carry the crystal. Keep the charged crystal with you throughout the lunar cycle as a reminder of your intentions and the spell's power.

Activate your warrior energy and move forward with the essence of Aries as a tool of empowerment this lunar cycle. This ritual amplifies your inner courage and provides you with just the right amount of fire to create the life you desire to live without burning out.

ARIES WAXING CRESCENT MOON

Plant Seeds of Action

ARIES WAXING CRESCENT MOON
QUICKIE
For the busiest of magical bees.

Busy Witch Ritual:

Identify small, actionable steps towards your intention. Use your morning routine to affirm these steps. A quick affirmation in the shower like, "I am taking charge of my dreams," can work wonders.

Self-Care Tip:

Do a five-minute meditation focusing on your breath to keep the fiery energy balanced.

Affirmation:

Under the Waxing Crescent Moon in Aries, I ignite the spark of my ambitions with unwavering determination. Each step I take is fueled by courage and clarity, propelling me towards my goals. I embrace the vibrant energy of Aries, allowing it to infuse my actions with confidence and vitality. With every breath, I draw in the strength to pursue my dreams and the resilience to overcome any obstacle. I am a dynamic force, steadily advancing on my path with the bold spirit of a warrior.

Aries Waxing Crescent Moon Ritual: Igniting Passion

♈

Harness the initiating energy of Aries during the waxing crescent phase of the Moon. Ignite your passions, set a clear intention for action, and begin manifesting your desires.

You Need:

- A red candle for the fiery energy of Aries.
- A ram figurine or image, symbolizing Aries.
- Crystals such as Red Jasper or Carnelian for courage and motivation.
- A small bowl of water to balance the fire energy.

To Begin:

- Create your sacred space by cleansing your space with smoke or sound to clear any stagnant energy. Envision any negativity or obstacles being removed, making way for new beginnings.
- Create a small altar with items that represent Aries energy.

The Ritual:

- Light your candle. As you light the candle, focus on its flame and invite the bold and assertive energy of Aries into your space.
- Set your ritual intention. Write your goal and intention on a piece of paper along with specific ways you want to initiate or act upon this during this lunar phase. Aries energy is all about taking decisive action, so be bold in your aspirations.

- Charge your crystal. Hold the Red Jasper or Carnelian in your hands, close your eyes, and visualize your goal and intention being infused into the crystal. Feel the energy of Aries - assertive, fiery, and courageous - charging the crystal.
- Speak your intention and action steps out loud with confidence. Use affirmations that resonate with Aries energy, like:
  - "I am bold and courageous in pursuing my goals."
  - "With every step, I confidently move towards my desires."
  - "I embrace the dynamic energy of Aries to initiate positive change in my life."
- Spend a few minutes meditating on your intention and actions. Visualize yourself taking action and moving forward with determination and courage. Feel the energy of the waxing crescent moon amplifying your desires.
- When you're ready, dip your fingers in the bowl of water and anoint your forehead, heart, and wrists. This act symbolizes the balance of fiery Aries energy with emotional clarity and calm.
- Thank the energies of Aries and the Moon for their guidance and support. Blow out the candle or let it burn out safely. Keep the charged crystal with you or place it on your altar as a reminder of your intention and action steps.

After the ritual, take one small but concrete step towards your intention within the next day. This aligns with Aries' call to action and begins the manifestation process.

The energy of Aries is bold and active, urging you to move forward with confidence and determination. Utilize this ritual to ignite your inner flame and move forward with confidence.

ARIES FIRST QUARTER MOON
Challenge Yourself

☽ ☽ ☽

ARIES FIRST QUARTER MOON
QUICKIE
For the busiest of magical bees.

Busy Witch Ritual:

Tackle a challenge related to your intention. Break it into manageable tasks. Even if it's a five minute task, dedicate this time to advance your goal and connect back to your intention.

Self-Care Tip:

Participate in a short, invigorating workout or a dance session to release stress and boost confidence.

Affirmation:

In this phase of action and challenge, I lovingly affirm my strength and determination. I nurture my body with vigor, my mind with positivity, and my soul with unwavering self-love. I am unstoppable, not just in pursuing my dreams, but in cherishing the sacred essence that is my being. I take action to feel the way I want to feel with passion.

Aries First Quarter Moon Ritual: Cultivating Courage

This ritual taps into the assertive and energetic vibes of Aries during the first quarter moon phase, a time traditionally associated with action, challenge, and building momentum.

You Need:
- A red or orange candle to symbolize the fiery spirit of Aries.
- Aries symbols, such as a ram figurine or images representing strength and bravery.
- Crystals like Bloodstone or Garnet for courage and resilience.
- A small bowl of water to balance the fire energy.
- A feather.

To Begin:
- Begin by using smoke to energetically clear your space, setting a focused atmosphere. Visualize the smoke carrying away any doubts or fears, leaving a space of potential and power.
- Create a small altar with items that represent Aries energy.

The Ritual:
- Light your candle. As you light your candle, focus on its warm, energetic flame. Invite the bold, assertive energy of Aries to infuse your ritual.

- Reflect on the goal and intention you set during the New Moon. Reaffirm the goals or intention, speaking them aloud with conviction. Aries energy favors bold, decisive action, so be clear and assertive in your words.
- Hold your chosen crystal in your hands. Visualize it absorbing the fiery energy of Aries, empowering you with the courage to face challenges and the strength to pursue your goal relentlessly.
- Close your eyes and meditate on any obstacles you face. Visualize the Aries ram, powerful and unstoppable, charging through these barriers. Feel yourself embodying this unstoppable force, breaking through anything that stands in your way.
- Repeat affirmations that resonate with Aries' fearless nature, such as
    - "I am empowered by the bold energy of Aries to overcome all obstacles."
    - "With courage and determination, I move forward towards my goals."
    - "I embrace challenges as opportunities for growth and strength."
- Dip the feather in the bowl of water and gently sprinkle drops around your altar and over your head. This act symbolizes the balance of fiery determination with the fluidity of emotion, bringing them into harmony.
- Write down one immediate, actionable step you can take in the next day to advance your intention. Aries energy is all about immediate action, so commit to this step as part of the ritual.
- Thank the energies of Aries and the Moon for their guidance. Extinguish the candle, or let it burn safely. Place the charged crystal in a prominent place as a reminder of your commitment.

This First Quarter Moon ritual in Aries is a powerful way to activate your inner warrior, face challenges head-on, and keep the momentum going with your goal and intention.

ARIES WAXING GIBBOUS MOON

Refine and Trust

ARIES WAXING GIBBOUS MOON
QUICKIE
For the busiest of magical bees.

Busy Witch Ritual:

Journal and remind yourself of the 'why' behind your intention and goal and feel the why in your body.

Self-Care Tip:

Take a warm, relaxing bath with a few drops of ginger tea or essence to keep the Aries fire alive but soothing.

Affirmation:

Under the Waxing Gibbous Moon in Aries, I harness its energy to refine and elevate my self-trust. With the fiery spirit of Aries guiding me, I affirm my commitment to personal growth and transformation. I am the embodiment of strength and determination, radiating confidence in every aspect of my life. I do what it takes to feel the way I want to feel and trust all is coming at just the right time.

Aries Waxing Gibbous Moon Ritual: Sigil Magic

This ritual harnesses the assertive energy of Aries in a phase that symbolizes refinement, adjustment, and preparation for culmination. Incorporating sigil making, it aims to empower your goal and intention with focused energy.

You Need:
- A red candle for Aries' passion and drive.
- Symbols of Aries, like a ram or images of Mars.
- Crystals such as Amethyst or Clear Quartz for clarity and strength.
- A bowl of water to balance the intensity of fire.

To Begin:
- Begin by using smoke to energetically clear your space, setting a focused atmosphere. Visualize the smoke carrying away any doubts or fears, leaving a space of potential and power.
- Create a small altar with items that represent Aries energy

The Ritual:
- Light your candle. As you light the candle, focus on its flame. Invite the bold, assertive energy of Aries to guide your ritual.
- Reflect on your intention, phrasing it in a positive, present tense.
- Write down your intention, then remove all vowels and duplicate consonants, leaving a string of unique letters.

- Creatively combine these letters into a sigil, a symbolic representation of your intention. Let your intuition guide the design.
- As you draw, infuse the sigil with your desire and the fiery energy of Aries.
- Hold the sigil in your hands and visualize it glowing with red, fiery energy.
- Affirm its power, saying, "With this sigil, I harness the energy of Aries to manifest my intention."
- Meditate while focusing on the sigil. Visualize your intention coming to fruition, empowered by the waxing gibbous moon and Aries' energy.
- Feel the excitement and anticipation of your impending success.
- Dip your fingers in the bowl of water and lightly touch your forehead, heart, and the sigil. This act balances the fiery energy with emotional clarity.
- Thank the energies of Aries and the Moon for their guidance.
- Extinguish the candle, or let it burn safely.
- Place the sigil in a prominent place where you'll see it often, like your altar or a journal.
- In alignment with Aries' proactive nature, plan an immediate action related to your intention. Commit to taking this step within the next 24 hours.

This Waxing Gibbous Moon ritual in Aries, enhanced with the creation and empowerment of a personal sigil, is a potent way to focus your will and prepare for the manifestation of your desires. The sigil serves as a tangible representation of your intention, charged with the fiery energy of Aries and the growing power of the moon.

ARIES
FULL MOON
Celebrate and Reflect

ARIES FULL MOON
QUICKIE
For the busiest of magical bees.

Busy Witch Ritual:

Hold a lit candle and acknowledge your progress. Celebrate your wins, no matter how small. Blow the candle out in celebration and reflection.

Self-Care Tip:

Practice journaling under the moonlight to fill your spiritual cup and dance with the power of Aries to fill your physical self-care cup, attend a sauna, or enjoy a night snuggled up with a heating pad to release what needs releasing.

Affirmation:

Under the Aries Full Moon, I bask in the glory of my achievements and the strength of my will. I celebrate the fiery energy that propels me forward, honoring the bold spirit within me that dares to dream and achieve. With the full moon's light as my guide, I recognize my courage, embrace my power, and revel in the victories of my journey. I make space to feel the way I want to feel.

Aries Full Moon Ritual: Shaking Off Limitations

This ritual is designed to embrace the energetic spirit of the Aries Full Moon. It focuses on releasing any limitations or obstacles that hinder your path, using the physical act of 'shaking it off' to symbolize liberation and renewal.

You Need:
- A red or white candle to symbolize the full moon and Aries' fiery energy.
- Symbols of Aries, such as a ram or images representing courage and strength.
- Crystals like Red Jasper or hematite for grounding and empowerment.
- A bowl of water with a pinch of ginger or black pepper for added fire energy.

To Begin:
- Begin by energetically clearing your space. As you do this, set the intention to clear away any negative energy, creating a space for empowerment and release.
- Create a small altar with items that represent Aries energy.

The Ritual:
- Light your candle and focus on its flame and invite the bold, assertive energy of Aries into your space.

- Reflect on what you wish to release. What limitations, fears, or obstacles are you facing? Write them down on a piece of paper.
- Stand comfortably with your feet shoulder-width apart.
- Begin to gently shake your body, starting from your feet and moving upwards. Let the movement be loose and freeing.
- As you shake, visualize shaking off all the limitations and obstacles you've identified. Imagine them falling away from your body, leaving you lighter and more empowered.
- Increase the intensity of your shaking as you feel comfortable, letting go of more and more baggage.
- After a few minutes, gradually slow down your shaking, coming back to stillness.
- With your feet firmly planted on the ground, hands on your hips, and eyes closed, repeat an empowering affirmation, such as:
  - "I release all that no longer serves me. I am strong, free, and empowered under this Aries Full Moon."
- Safely burn the paper with your written limitations (perhaps over the bowl of water or in a fire-safe container). As it burns, imagine those limitations being transformed into smoke and disappearing into the air.
- Thank the energies of Aries and the Full Moon for their strength and clarity.
- Extinguish the candle safely.
- To conclude, ground yourself by eating something, taking deep breaths, or visualizing roots growing from your feet into the earth.

This ritual is a powerful way to actively engage with and release the barriers that hold you back, using the energetic and transformative power of the Aries Full Moon to propel you forward into a state of renewed strength.

ARIES WANING GIBBOUS MOON

Share Your Fire

☽ ☽ ☽

ARIES WANING GIBBOUS MOON
QUICKIE
For the busiest of magical bees.

Busy Witch Ritual:

Give back to yourself by going through a closet or drawer and doing a vibe check. If it's not "the vibe," let it go.

Self-Care Tip:

Engage in a hobby that lights up your soul and release any guilt associated with it.

Affirmation:

I gracefully embrace the art of letting go. I release what no longer serves my spirit, making room for growth and renewal. With the courage of Aries as my guide, I trust in the natural cycle of release and rebirth. I acknowledge my achievements and learn from my challenges, using them as stepping stones to greater heights. In this phase of reflection and gratitude, I honor my journey, understanding that every experience has contributed to my strength and resilience.

Aries Waning Gibbous Moon Ritual: Self-Reflection and Gratitude

Leverage the introspective energy of this moon phase. By simply sitting and observing oneself in a mirror, surrounded by the gentle light of candles, this ritual encourages a deep and appreciative connection with your inner self.

You Need:
- A mirror.
- Candles.

To Begin:
- Begin by clearing your space with smoke or sound. As you cleanse, set an intention for clarity and self-acceptance.
- Arrange a comfortable space where you can sit undisturbed in front of a mirror.
- Place a few candles around the mirror in a safe manner, ensuring that the flickering light can be seen in the mirror's reflection.

The Ritual:
- Light the candles around the mirror, focusing on the intention of illuminating your inner self. The fire's energy, resonating with Aries, will aid in burning away self-doubt and illuminating your true essence.
- Sit comfortably in front of the mirror, allowing yourself to relax and breathe deeply.

- Gaze into your own eyes in the mirror. Let your gaze be soft and accepting.
- As you look at your reflection, allow your thoughts to wander. Observe them without judgment, letting them flow freely.
- Notice the way the candlelight dances and reflects in the mirror, creating a mesmerizing, meditative state.
- Begin to shift your thoughts towards gratitude. Think about the aspects of yourself for which you are thankful.
- Acknowledge your strengths, your journey, and even your flaws, understanding that they all contribute to who you are.
- Whisper words of gratitude and acceptance to your reflection. You might say, "I am grateful for my strength," or "I accept myself fully."
- Continue to gaze into the mirror, allowing a sense of peace and self-compassion to wash over you.
- If emotions arise, let them flow. This is a safe space for you to confront and embrace all aspects of yourself.
- Once the candles have burned down significantly, or you feel your ritual is complete, gently close the ritual.
- Thank the energies of Aries and the Moon for their guidance in this self-discovery experience and extinguish the candles safely.
- After the ritual, take some time to journal about your experience. Write down any insights, emotions, or revelations that came up during your mirror gazing.

This Disseminating Moon in Aries ritual is a powerful exercise in self-reflection and gratitude. It encourages you to confront and embrace all aspects of your being, fostering a deeper understanding and appreciation of yourself.

ARIES THIRD QUARTER MOON

Release and Let Go

ARIES THIRD QUARTER MOON

QUICKIE
For the busiest of magical bees.

Busy Witch Ritual:

Identify what hasn't served you in this cycle. Consciously let go of these elements. Declutter your life and mind.

Self-Care Tip:

Spend time doing some simple decluttering, be it your workspace or digital space, to create room for new energy.

Affirmation:

In the reflective light of the Aries Third Quarter Moon, I embrace the power of my future vision. I release old patterns with courage, making space for new growth. My spirit is resilient, ready for the next chapter with a renewed fire and clarity. I dream as if I can do and be anything, with confidence and high energy.

Aries Third Quarter Moon Ritual: Release and Realign

♈

Aries, with its fiery and assertive energy, encourages decisive action and letting go of what no longer serves your highest purpose. Boldly confront and release those aspects of your life that are holding you back.

You Need:
- A red candle for courage and initiative.
- Symbols of Aries, like a ram or images representing strength and assertiveness.
- Crystals such as Black Obsidian or Hematite for grounding and protection.
- A bowl of water with a pinch of salt for purification.

To Begin:
- Begin by energetically clearing your space. As you cleanse, envision any stagnant energies or obstacles being cleared away, creating a space of power and possibility.
- Arrange your altar with items that resonate with Aries' fiery energy.

The Ritual:
- As you light the candle, focus on its flame. Invite the bold, assertive energy of Aries to guide your ritual.

- Take a moment to reflect on what you need to release. What habits, thoughts, or situations are no longer serving you? Write these down on a piece of paper.
- Stand up and read aloud what you've written, acknowledging these aspects of your life in an assertive act of release.
- Then, declare your intention to release them. You might say, "I now let go of these burdens, freeing myself for new growth."
- Tear up the paper as a symbol of your commitment to release and move on.
- Dip your fingers in the bowl of salt water.
- Anoint your forehead, heart, and wrists, symbolizing the cleansing of mind, emotions, and actions.
- Visualize the salt water absorbing and neutralizing any residual negativity or attachments.
- Sit comfortably and hold your grounding crystal.
- Close your eyes and visualize roots extending from your feet deep into the earth.
- With each breath, feel more grounded and centered, ready to move forward with clarity and purpose.
- Thank the energies of Aries and the Moon for their strength and guidance.
- Extinguish the candle safely.
- Dispose of the torn paper pieces outside, returning them to the earth.
- In alignment with Aries' proactive nature, identify a positive action you can take immediately to step into this new phase of release and renewal.

Actively engage with and release the barriers that hold you back using the energetic and transformative power of Aries to propel you forward into a state of renewed strength and determination.

ARIES WANING CRESCENT MOON

Rest and Retrospect

ARIES WANING CRESCENT MOON
QUICKIE
For the busiest of magical bees.

Busy Witch Ritual:

Slow down. Reflect on the cycle and how it has impacted your life. Start thinking about what you want for the next cycle. Consider creating a list of feeling words.

Self-Care Tip:

Enjoy a quiet evening with a book or a gentle yoga session to wind down and turn inwards, laying the Aries energy to rest.

Affirmation:

As the Waning Crescent Moon in Aries fades, I too let go of what no longer serves me. I embrace calm and renewal, preparing for new beginnings with courage and an open heart. My inner warrior is ready to retreat and make space for the grounding earthy energy to come in the next lunar cycle. As I grow, the warrior in me also grows.

Aries Waning Crescent Moon Ritual: Candle Cleansing

♈

It's time for energy clearing, reflection, and preparation for the new cycle. The candle cleansing technique used in this ritual symbolizes the purging of old energies and the transformation of these into positive, rejuvenating forces.

You Need:
- A white spell candle.
- Any items that represent Aries.

To Begin:
- Clear your area with smoke, sound, or your preferred method. Set the intention for a safe, sacred space where you can release and renew.
- Arrange a comfortable space with minimal distractions. Place a white spell candle at the center, symbolizing clarity, peace, and the transformative fire of Aries.

The Ritual:
- Hold the white spell candle in your hands for a few moments. Close your eyes and set your intention for this ritual - to release all that no longer serves you and to welcome transformation and renewal.
- Begin at the crown of your head, gently rolling the candle over your scalp.

- Slowly move the candle down your face, visualizing any negative thoughts or stress melting away and adhering to the candle's wax.
- Continue down your body, front and back, arms, and legs. Be thorough but gentle, covering as much of your body as you comfortably can.
- With each pass of the candle, imagine it absorbing stagnant energies, worries, and any blockages that hinder your progress.
- As you perform the candle cleansing, visualize the negative energies being drawn out of your body and into the candle. See them as dark smudges or smoke being trapped in the wax.
- Feel yourself becoming lighter, clearer, and more at peace with each roll of the candle.
- Once you feel the cleansing is complete, light the candle.
- As it burns, watch the flame and know that the negative energies are being transformed. Envision them being released into the universe, where they are transmuted into positive, healing energy.
- Sit quietly, observing the flame, and bask in the sense of release and clarity.
- Thank the energies of Aries and the Balsamic Moon for their guidance and transformative power.
- Allow the candle to burn out safely, or if necessary, extinguish it with gratitude.
- Spend some time in quiet reflection or meditation, embracing the calm and clarity brought by the ritual.
- Drink some water or herbal tea to help ground yourself.

This Aries Waning Crescent Moon ritual is a powerful way to engage with the introspective energy of this lunar phase, using the transformative fire of Aries to clarify and prepare for the new cycle.

ARIES RITUAL NOTES

ARIES RITUAL NOTES

TAURUS

Taurus, the second sign of the zodiac, is the embodiment of stability, persistence, and a deep connection to the sensual pleasures of life. Taurus brings the energy of grounding yourself, nurturing growth, and appreciating the beauty of the journey. When the Moon is in Taurus during its various phases, it invites you to slow down, root deeply into your intentions, and cultivate your desires with a steady, unwavering focus in the midst of life's chaos. Taurus energy is both calming and enduring.

However, let's acknowledge the flip side – sometimes the steadfast nature of Taurus can lead to a bit of stubbornness, making it challenging to adapt to change or let go of what's comfortable (even the most patient gardeners sometimes struggle to prune their beloved plants).

Just as Taurus energy can provide a comforting sense of stability, it can also lead to a sense of stagnation. This is an energy that many busy individuals might find familiar. What starts as a commitment to a routine or a cherished project can sometimes turn into a reluctance to venture into uncharted territory or the unknown.

Taurus Moon Toolkit

Here are some suggested tools for your Taurus moon ritual kit. Keep in mind that everything is optional and the only true requirement is your energy, magic, and belief!

- Sun Sign Dates: April 20-May 20

- Candle Color: Green

- Oil or Essence: Rose (for love and grounding)

- Herb: Mint (for abundance and sensuality)

- Spell Focus: Stability and patience

- Element: Earth   Tarot: Pentacles

- Crystal: Rose Quartz

- Mythology: Venus or Zeus

Taurus In My Chart

Refer to your birth chart and look for Taurus. It may be
marked with this symbol: ♉

🌙 **House(s):**

🌙 **Planet(s):**

🌙 **Notes:**

Whenever the Moon is in Taurus, it will highlight this part
of your birth chart and you may notice heightened
emotions in this area or shadow aspects of your life or
energy coming to the surface.

TAURUS NEW MOON
Set Intention with Stability

TAURUS NEW MOON
QUICKIE
For the busiest of magical bees.

Busy Witch Ritual:

Find a quiet moment to ground yourself. Write down a practical action step that brings more stability into your life and helps you feel the way you want to feel.

Self-Care Tip:

Take a short nature walk to connect with the earth and solidify your intention and/or goal.

Affirmation:

Under the grounding New Moon in Taurus, I plant the seeds of stability and growth. With every deep breath, I draw in abundance and nurture my intention and goal with patience and perseverance. I am rooted in my purpose, flourishing in harmony with nature's rhythms. I am rooted and steadfast.

Taurus New Moon Ritual: Grounding Meditation

Utilizing grounding meditation, this ritual helps you connect deeply with the earth, anchoring your intention and goal in the physical realm and drawing upon the nurturing, steadfast energy of Taurus.

You Need:

- Cedar or sandalwood incense or essence.
- Calming music that resonates with you.
- Two grounding crystals such as Red Jasper or Black Tourmaline.

To Begin:

- Light the incense and turn on the music.
- Lie down comfortably on the ground, preferably in a quiet, peaceful spot. Close your eyes and hold one crystal in each hand, feeling their weight and presence.

The Ritual:

- As you lie still, focus on the sensation of your body against the ground.
- Visualize energetic roots extending from your entire backside, penetrating deep into the earth. Feel the stability and nurturing energy of the earth.
- Allow these roots to spread and intertwine with the earth's core, grounding you firmly and securely.

- With your body grounded, bring your intention for this moon cycle to mind.
- Visualize your intention clearly, feeling the emotions and desires associated with it. Let this feeling permeate your entire being, growing in strength.
- As the feeling intensifies, envision your energy rising upwards, reaching out towards the universe. Imagine your intention being heard and acknowledged by the universe.
- Rest in this space of connection and receptivity for a while, connecting your intention with the universe's energy.
- When you feel ready, gently begin to draw your energy back into your body. Visualize pulling strength and nourishment up from the earth and drawing inspiration and cosmic energy down from above. Feel yourself filled with a beautifully grounded yet expansive energy.
- Slowly start to wiggle your toes and fingers, bringing gentle movement back into your body. When you feel ready, gently sit up, taking a moment to acclimate to your surroundings.
- Thank the energies of Taurus and the New Moon for their guidance and support.
- Extinguish the incense. Reflect on your experience in a journal, noting any insights or feelings that arose.
- Carry or wear the grounding crystals you used in the ritual as a reminder of your intentions and connection to the earth.

Plant the seeds of your desires, trusting in the stable, fertile ground of Taurus to bring them to fruition. Grounding meditation is a wonderful way to anchor into your desires and reset your energy from the experience of day to day life that distracts you from feeling the way you want to feel.

TAURUS WAXING CRESCENT MOON

Embody Your Intention

TAURUS
WAXING CRESCENT MOON
QUICKIE
For the busiest of magical bees.

Busy Witch Ritual:

Choose one or two small, nurturing steps to take to feel the way you want to feel. Incorporate these into your daily routine, like a morning affirmation or a healthy breakfast.

Self-Care Tip:

Garden or care for houseplants to physically connect with the process and energy of nurturing and tending.

Affirmation:

As the Waxing Crescent Moon glows in steadfast Taurus, I embrace the nurturing energy of growth and stability. With each step, I build a foundation of abundance and security, trusting in the steady progress of my dreams. I am grounded and flourishing as I cultivate my intentions with patience and persistence.

Taurus Waxing Crescent Moon Ritual: The Five Senses

Taurus invites us to connect deeply with our desires and begin manifesting them in the physical world. By engaging all five senses, this ritual aims to solidify your intention and align your actions with how you want to feel, making your desire a tangible reality.

You Need:
- Paper and pen for writing your intention and goal.
- Something aromatic that resonates with your intention.
- Music that matches the theme or energy of your intention.
- Additional items to engage your other senses, such as a favorite snack (taste), a tactile object (touch), and an image or object (sight).

To Begin:
- Write down the intention you set during the New Moon. Be clear and specific (choose one now if you didn't decide then).
- Also, jot down actionable steps you plan to take as the moon moves towards the First Quarter phase.

The Ritual:
- Turn on your chosen music. Let it fill your space, creating an energy that aligns with your intention.
- Sit comfortably and hold your written intention to your lower belly area, then your heart.

- Close your eyes and take a few deep breaths, centering yourself.
- Reflect on your intention: What does it look like in action? How does it feel to move towards this goal? Are your steps aligned with your true desires?
- Allow yourself to ask difficult questions, using Taurus' supportive energy to seek honest answers. Journal if you'd like.
- Engage Your Senses:
    - Smell: Let the smell of your chosen aromatic envelop you, linking the scent to your intention.
    - Hearing: Focus on the music, letting it inspire and motivate you.
    - Taste: Have a small bite of your chosen snack, connecting the flavor to the sweetness of achieving your goals.
    - Touch: Hold the tactile object, feeling its texture and relating it to the physicality of your intentions.
    - Sight: Gaze at your chosen image or object, visualizing your intention coming to life.
- Consider how you can incorporate these sensory elements into your daily life. For instance, carry the herb blend with you, listen to the theme music during your morning routine, or place the visual object where you'll see it often.
- Thank the energies of Taurus and the Waxing Crescent Moon for their guidance.
- Reflect on how each sense contributed to a deeper understanding and connection with your intention and goal.
- Keep engaging with your chosen sensory elements regularly to reinforce your intention.

Ground your intentions in the physical world, using the power of the senses to solidify and manifest your desires. By engaging sight, sound, smell, taste, and touch, you create a multi-sensory experience that anchors your intention in reality.

TAURUS FIRST QUARTER MOON

Build Steadily

☽ ☽ ☽

TAURUS FIRST QUARTER MOON
QUICKIE
For the busiest of magical bees.

Busy Witch Ritual:

Dedicate time over the next three days to work toward your goal and intention. And so it is.

Self-Care Tip:

Enjoy a relaxing massage or self-massage to release tension and maintain focus.

Affirmation:

Under the First Quarter Moon in resilient Taurus, I find strength in my resolve. I take decisive steps towards my goal and intention, grounded in the certainty of my purpose. With each action, I lay another brick on the path of my aspirations, building a future of abundance and fulfillment. I trust that I am taking the action I need to take in order to feel the way I want to feel.

Taurus First Quarter Moon Ritual: Resource Integration

Taurus, known for its practicality and affinity for material comfort, guides us in integrating our intentions into our lives by effectively utilizing and acquiring the necessary resources.

You Need:
- A sheet of paper and a pen.
- A comfortable and quiet space where you can think and plan without interruption.

To Begin:
- At the top of your paper, write down the intention you set during the New Moon. Keep it clear and concise.

The Ritual:
- Divide the paper into two columns.
- In the first column, list all the tools, resources, and support systems you believe are necessary to realize your intention. Think broadly – this can include physical items, financial resources, emotional support, information, skills, and connections.
- In the second column, outline how you plan to acquire or access these resources. Be as specific as possible. For example, if you need financial resources, detail how you will budget, save, or earn the necessary funds.

- Remember that time and energy are crucial resources. Reflect on how you can allocate your time and maintain your energy levels to support your intention.
- Write down any adjustments you might need to make in your daily routine or lifestyle to ensure you have the time and energy for your goal.
- Acknowledge the importance of physical and mental health in realizing your intention.
- Note down any health-related actions or routines you need to adopt or maintain. This could include exercise, nutrition, rest, or stress management techniques.
- Review your plan and feel the grounded, nurturing energy of Taurus infusing it with practicality and resilience.
- Fold the paper and place it somewhere you will see it often, such as your workspace or a personal altar.
- Thank the energies of Taurus and the First Quarter Moon for their guidance and support.
- Begin to implement your plan. Take small, consistent steps towards gathering your resources and aligning your lifestyle with your intention.

This First Quarter Moon in Taurus ritual is a powerful way to ground your intentions in practical action, ensuring you have the necessary resources, time, and energy to bring your desires to fruition.
By planning and preparing in alignment with Taurus' stable, resourceful energy, you set a strong foundation for the manifestation of your goals.

TAURUS WAXING GIBBOUS MOON
Refine and Connect

TAURUS
WAXING GIBBOUS MOON
QUICKIE
For the busiest of magical bees.

Busy Witch Ritual:

Light a candle and release any expectations you're holding. Refresh a cozy spot in your home to deepen into the present.

Self-Care Tip:

Take a luxurious bath with earthy bath herbs to stay grounded and patient.

Affirmation:

As the Waxing Gibbous Moon in Taurus brightens the sky, I embrace its nurturing energy. I trust in the steady growth of my goal and intention, grounded in the earth's wisdom. My efforts are fruitful, and my path is clear. I am patient, persistent, and aligned with the abundance of the universe. I trust that I am capable of feeling the way I want to feel.

Taurus Waxing Gibbous Moon Ritual: Earth Connection

Reconnect with the Earth and embrace Taurus' affinity for nature and grounding. This ritual focuses on finding beauty and tranquility in the natural world, trusting in the universe's timing, and tuning into the subtle messages it offers.

You Need (choose depending on the activity you will do):

- You might need gardening tools, comfortable walking shoes, a blanket for lying down, or just yourself.

To Begin:

- Once you're in your chosen outdoor setting, take a moment to breathe deeply and center yourself.
- Engage in your chosen activity, be it gardening, walking, meditating, or simply sitting. Let this action be gentle and unhurried.

The Ritual:

- As you connect with the Earth, open your senses to your surroundings. Notice the textures, colors, sounds, and scents around you.
- If you're walking, feel each step and how the earth supports you. If you're gardening, notice the feel of the soil and the life it nurtures. If you're lying down, observe the clouds and how they morph and drift.

- If it's sunny, take a moment to bask in the sunlight. Feel its warmth on your skin and envision it energizing and revitalizing you.
- If possible, lean against a tree or place your feet in water. Feel the solid strength of the tree or the fluidity of the water, and allow these elements to ground you further.
- Acknowledge the Yin energy of both the Waxing Gibbous Moon and Taurus. Allow yourself to be receptive and open to the universe's wisdom.
- Ask yourself or the universe any questions you have been pondering. Listen quietly for any insights or intuitions that arise.
- Thank the Earth, the Moon, and Taurus for their grounding energy and the insights provided.
- Take a few deep breaths, grounding yourself once more before leaving your outdoor space.
- Reflect on any insights or feelings that arose during your time in nature. You may wish to journal these.
- In the days leading up to the Full Moon, continue to reflect on these insights and how they relate to your current intentions or path.

This Waxing Gibbous Moon in Taurus ritual is a beautiful way to reconnect with the Earth, embracing the grounding and nurturing qualities of nature. It's a time to slow down, appreciate the beauty of the practical world, and listen to the subtle messages of the universe, aligning yourself with its perfect timing.

TAURUS FULL MOON
Compost and Appreciate

TAURUS FULL MOON
QUICKIE
For the busiest of magical bees.

Busy Witch Ritual:

Reflect on all that you've harvested this cycle. Cheers yourself!

Self-Care Tip:

Prepare a special meal or treat yourself to something that delights your senses.

Affirmation:

Under the luminous Taurus Full Moon, I celebrate the blossoming of my efforts. I am grounded in gratitude, surrounded by abundance and beauty. My heart and soul are in harmony with nature's enduring strength. I embrace the fullness of my achievements with joy and thankfulness. I release resistance to feeling the way I want to feel and am comfortable embracing the transformation.

Taurus Full Moon Ritual: Compost Resistance

This ritual takes advantage of the nurturing earth energy of Taurus and the illuminating power of the Full Moon to compost a physical representation of your current resistance. This ritual symbolizes the release of barriers, blending earth magic with manifestation.

You Need:
- Select a plant that resonates with your intention. Research plants with magical properties that align with what you wish to manifest or release.
- A pot or a chosen spot in your garden.
- Suitable soil for your plant.
- A piece of paper and a pen.
- Gardening tools as needed.

To Begin:
- On the piece of paper, write down what you want to manifest or release. Be clear and specific. For example, "I release my fear and grow in confidence."
- If using a pot, fill it partly with soil. If planting outdoors, choose a spot where your plant will thrive, considering sunlight and soil conditions.

The Ritual:

- Place your written release at the bottom of the pot or in your chosen spot in the ground.
- Gently place your plant on top and cover the roots with more soil. As you do this, visualize your intention taking root and growing with the plant. Visualize your resistance composting and turning into nutrients for the plant.
- Once your plant is securely in place, take a moment under the Full Moon to connect with its energy.
- Hold your hands over the plant and envision the Full Moon's light bathing the plant and your intention in a nurturing glow.
- Affirm the growth of your intention, saying something like, "As this plant grows, so too does my intention manifest."
- Water your plant gently, imagining the water as nourishment for your intention.
- As you water, think about how you will nurture and tend to your intention in your daily life, just as you will care for the plant.
- Thank the energies of Taurus and the Full Moon for their support.
- Keep track of your plant's growth and reflect on the parallel growth or manifestation of your intention.

This Taurus Full Moon ritual is a beautiful blend of practical gardening and magical intention-setting. It's a powerful way to physically and symbolically plant your desires, allowing them to grow and manifest in alignment with the nurturing energy of Taurus and the bright illumination of the Full Moon.

TAURUS WANING GIBBOUS MOON

Gratitude For Your Bounty

TAURUS
WANING GIBBOUS MOON
QUICKIE
For the busiest of magical bees.

Busy Witch Ritual:

Journal on all that you've received this cycle and identify one thing (physically or emotionally) you'd like to give to someone else. Then do it!

Self-Care Tip:

Cook a meal with fresh produce that was locally grown, if possible.

Affirmation:

As the Taurus Waning Gibbous Moon wanes, I release attachments to material desires, embracing simplicity and contentment. I trust in the natural flow of giving and receiving, finding balance and peace in letting go. My spirit is enriched by gratitude and grounded in the Earth's wisdom. I am steady and strong in my ability to feel the way I want to feel.

Taurus Waning Gibbous Moon Ritual: Gaia Gratitude

Express gratitude and connect with the Earth. Taurus reminds us of the nurturing and sustaining power of Mother Earth, Gaia. This ritual involves activities that honor Gaia, fostering a sense of gratitude and interconnectedness with nature, and allowing the stresses of modern life to fade.

You Need:

- Gather natural elements such as stones, leaves, flowers, or fruits to create an altar that honors Gaia.

To Begin:

- Decide on how you wish to connect with nature. Options include creating a nature mandala, planting a tree, sprinkling wildflower seeds, making a bird feeder, or simply walking barefoot on the earth or dipping your feet in water.
- Set up your natural altar, arranging the elements in a way that feels harmonious and beautiful. As you do this, reflect on the abundance and beauty that Gaia provides.

The Ritual:

- Engage in your chosen activity. If you're creating a mandala, focus on the symmetry and balance of nature. If planting seeds, consider the growth these plants will bring. If making a bird feeder, think about the joy and sustenance you're providing to local wildlife.

- If you choose to eat fruits or vegetables, do so mindfully. With each bite, express your gratitude to Gaia for the nourishment and abundance she provides.
- If near a body of water, place your feet in it. Feel your connection to this essential element, recognizing that water is a source of life and a part of you.
- Sit comfortably, either by your altar or in your chosen natural setting. Close your eyes and take deep, grounding breaths.
- Reflect on the gifts of nature and the Earth. Express your gratitude for the air you breathe, the food you eat, the beauty you witness, and the water that sustains you.
- Visualize this gratitude as a warm, glowing light radiating from your heart, spreading into the earth, and connecting you with Gaia.
- Thank Gaia and the energies of Taurus and the Disseminating Moon for their nurturing presence and the peace they bring.
- Take a few more deep breaths, grounding yourself and carrying this sense of gratitude and connection with you.
- Whenever you feel stressed, recall this sense of connection and gratitude to realign with the calming energy of Gaia.

This Waning Gibbous Moon in Taurus ritual is a beautiful way to honor Gaia, expressing gratitude for her endless gifts. Remember your deep connection with the Earth, and the peace and grounding that this connection brings, especially in the hustle of modern life.

TAURUS THIRD QUARTER MOON
Release and Simplify

TAURUS THIRD QUARTER MOON
QUICKIE
For the busiest of magical bees.

Busy Witch Ritual:

Let go of what hasn't worked. Simplify your approach and focus on what truly matters. Drink a cup of tea to honor the simplicity.

Self-Care Tip:

Declutter your living space to create a peaceful and cozy environment.

Affirmation:

In the grounding light of the Taurus Third Quarter Moon, I embrace the power of release. I let go of what no longer serves me, making room for growth and renewal. My roots are deep in stability, and I trust in the steady process of transformation and growth.

Taurus Third Quarter Moon Ritual: Financial Abundance and Gratitude

Taurus, associated with material wealth and comfort, provides the perfect backdrop for acknowledging and appreciating the financial blessings in our lives, no matter how big or small.

You Need:
- A journal or notebook and a pen.
- A comfortable and quiet space where you can reflect and write.

To Begin:
- For a few days surrounding the Third Quarter Moon, commit to tracking every cent that comes into your life. This includes your regular income, any found money, gifts, discounts, or savings.
- Write down each instance of financial gain in your journal, no matter how small. Note the amount and the source.

The Ritual:
- Review your journal entries. Reflect on the financial abundance you've recorded.
- Acknowledge and express gratitude for each instance, recognizing it as a gift from the universe. You might say, "I am grateful for the abundance that flows into my life, in all its forms."
- Sit comfortably, close your eyes, and take a few deep breaths.

- Visualize yourself surrounded by a warm, golden light, symbolizing the abundance that envelops your life.
- Imagine this light growing brighter with each financial blessing you've noted, feeling a sense of gratitude and contentment.
- Continue your meditation with affirmations that reinforce your appreciation for financial abundance. Repeat phrases like, "I am open to the abundance of the universe," or, "I gratefully receive all the financial blessings in my life."
- Conclude your meditation and affirmations with a final statement of thanks to the universe for its continuous generosity.
- Close your journal and take a moment to bask in the feelings of gratitude and abundance.
- Continue tracking your financial blessings for an extended period. The longer you do this, the more you'll recognize and appreciate the abundance in your life.
- Share your abundance with others when you can, whether through charity, gifts, or acts of kindness, to keep the cycle of generosity flowing.

This Third Quarter Moon in Taurus ritual is a powerful way to cultivate a mindset of abundance and gratitude, particularly regarding finances. By acknowledging every instance of financial gain, no matter how small, you open yourself up to recognizing and appreciating the wealth that surrounds you, fostering a deeper connection with the generous energy of the universe.

TAURUS WANING CRESCENT MOON

Rest and Rejuvenate

TAURUS
WANING CRESCENT MOON
QUICKIE
For the busiest of magical bees.

Busy Witch Ritual:

Take time to rest and rejuvenate. Reflect on your journey and how it has grounded you. Take a sacred nap.

Self-Care Tip:

Create a quiet evening with a comforting ritual, like a cup of herbal tea and soft music.

Affirmation:

As the Taurus Waning Crescent Moon fades, I embrace the quiet moments of introspection. I trust in the natural cycle of renewal, preparing my heart and soul for new beginnings. Grounded in the earth's wisdom, I find peace in letting go and await the new cycle with open arms and a hopeful spirit.

Taurus Waning Crescent Moon Ritual: Abundance Awareness

Set intentions that will flourish over time. This ritual centers around recognizing and celebrating the abundance in your life, creating a positive and prosperous mindset for the new moon cycle ahead.

You Need:
- Choose a quiet and comfortable space for your ritual.
- Candles to create a warm and inviting ambiance.
- Play music that uplifts and soothes you.
- Arrange your favorite crystals, or burn incense with a scent that you find heavenly.

To Begin:
- Sit comfortably in your sacred space, taking a few deep breaths to center yourself.
- With a pen and paper, start listing all the ways in which you are abundant. This can include material possessions, relationships, experiences, talents, and internal qualities.

The Ritual:
- Allow yourself to deeply reflect on each aspect of abundance in your life. Feel gratitude for these blessings, recognizing how they enrich your life.

- As you write each item, pause to really feel the gratitude for it. Visualize how each aspect of abundance has positively impacted your life.
- Let this exercise be a celebration of all the good that surrounds you.
- Once you have completed your list, choose what you'd like to do with the paper (burn it, bury it, place it on a sacred space until the New Moon in just a few days, etc.).
- Sit quietly for a few moments, absorbing the feelings of abundance and gratitude.
- Thank the energies of Taurus and the Balsamic Moon for their grounding and enriching influence.
- Blow out the candles, or let them burn down safely, as you conclude your ritual.
- Whenever you encounter resistance or challenges in the upcoming cycle, recall the feelings of gratitude and abundance from this ritual. Use this energy to propel you forward with a positive mindset.

Acknowledge and celebrate the abundance in your life, setting a foundation of gratitude and prosperity for the upcoming lunar cycle. By focusing on the richness of your current experiences and blessings, you align yourself with Taurus' energy of growth and value, preparing to start the next cycle with a positive and abundant mindset.

TAURUS RITUAL NOTES

TAURUS RITUAL NOTES

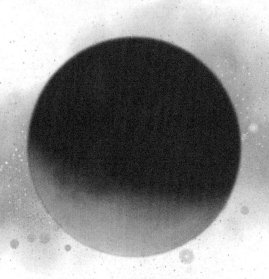

GEMINI

Gemini, the third sign of the zodiac, is the embodiment of adaptability, communication, and intellectual curiosity. When the Moon is in Gemini, it invites you to embrace flexibility, engage with your surroundings, and explore your ideas with a lively and open spirit.

Gemini energy is both stimulating and versatile. However, let's consider the other side of the coin – sometimes the mercurial nature of Gemini can lead to a scattering of energies, making it a challenge to stay focused or dive deeply into one area (even the most enthusiastic multitaskers can find themselves spread too thin).

Just as Gemini's energy can spark a delightful sense of curiosity and a thirst for variety, it can also lead to a sense of restlessness. What begins as a pursuit of multiple interests or a flurry of new ideas can sometimes evolve into a struggle to maintain consistency or see projects through to completion. Gemini's energy teaches us the importance of balance between embracing diverse experiences and maintaining a sense of direction. Sometimes the journey itself is as rewarding as the destination.

Gemini Moon Toolkit

Here are some suggested tools for your Gemini moon ritual kit. Keep in mind that everything is optional and the only true requirement is your energy, magic, and belief!

🌙 **Sun Sign Dates: May 21-June 20**

🌙 **Candle Color: Yellow**

🌙 **Oil or Essence: Lavender (for communication and calm)**

🌙 **Herb: Dill (for intellect and agility)**

🌙 **Spell Focus: Adaptability and learning**

🌙 **Element: Air**   🌙 **Tarot: Swords**

🌙 **Crystal: Tiger's Eye**

🌙 **Mythology: Castor and Pollux**

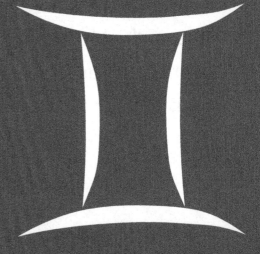

Gemini In My Chart

Refer to your birth chart and look for Gemini. It may be marked with this symbol: ♊

🌙 **House(s):**

🌙 **Planet(s):**

🌙 **Notes:**

Whenever the Moon is in Gemini, it will highlight this part of your birth chart. You may notice heightened emotions in this area or shadow aspects of your life or energy coming to the surface.

GEMINI
NEW MOON
Set Intention with Curiosity

GEMINI NEW MOON
QUICKIE
For the busiest of magical bees.

Busy Witch Ritual:

In a quiet moment, write down a goal that sparks your curiosity and desire for learning. How does this help you feel the way you want to feel?

Self-Care Tip:

A quick brainstorming session or journaling to explore your intention from different angles to clear your head.

Affirmation:

Under the Gemini New Moon, I embrace new beginnings with an open mind and a curious heart. I welcome fresh ideas and diverse perspectives, allowing them to ignite my creativity and guide my journey. In this cycle of renewal, I am ready to explore, communicate, and connect with the world around me in exciting and meaningful ways.

Gemini New Moon Ritual: Moon Circle

The Moon Circle is a sacred space for receiving guidance and clarity, helping you to set intentions that resonate deeply with your path for the upcoming lunar cycle.

You Need:
- Find a quiet, comfortable outdoor space where you can create your Moon Circle. Ensure it's a place where you can be undisturbed.
- Collect natural elements like stones or shells to mark your circle. You'll need four items for the cardinal points (North, South, East, West) and one for the center.

To Begin:
- Lay out your natural elements in a large circle on the ground. If it's a permanent circle, you can use more elements to define it.
- Mark the cardinal points within the circle, aligning them accurately with a compass if possible.
- Place a special item in the center of the circle, such as a plant, crystal, or statue, to focus the energy.

The Ritual:
- Before entering the circle, take a moment to ground yourself. Breathe deeply and visualize any external energies being released from your body.

- Step into the circle at the eastern point, symbolizing new beginnings and the rising sun.
- Begin to walk clockwise around the circle at least three times, focusing on your connection with the universe and your inner self.
- As you walk, pay attention to the rise in energy. When you feel a call to sit, do so and open yourself to any messages or guidance from the universe.
- Sit quietly, listening and feeling for any insights or intuitions that come to you.
- When ready, continue walking clockwise until you reach the western point, symbolizing completion and gratitude.
- Express your thanks to the universe or spirit for the guidance and presence.
- After exiting the circle, spend some time writing about your experience. Reflect on the intention you are considering and how you feel about it post-Moon Circle.
- Consider any changes or adjustments to your intention based on the messages or realizations received during the ritual.
- Keep the insights from your Moon Circle in mind as you move through the lunar cycle. Let them guide your actions and decisions.
- Consider making the Moon Circle a regular part of your New Moon practice, either alone or as part of a group ritual.

Circle is a powerful way to connect with your inner self and the universe, fostering a deeper understanding of your path and intention. By walking the circle and opening yourself to universal messages, you align your energy with that of Gemini.

GEMINI WAXING CRESCENT MOON
Communicate Your Vision

GEMINI
WAXING CRESCENT MOON
QUICKIE
For the busiest of magical bees.

Busy Witch Ritual:

Share your intention with a friend for accountability or write it down in a creative way. Use communication as a tool to give life to your goal and/or intention.

Self-Care Tip:

Practice relational self-care by meeting with a friend and enjoying laughter and good, refreshing conversation.

Affirmation:

As the Waxing Crescent Moon shines in Gemini, I harness the power of communication and adaptability. I am open to learning, growing, and embracing change with ease. My thoughts are clear, my words are powerful, and I confidently express my true self, ready to embrace the opportunities that come my way.

Gemini Waxing Crescent Moon Ritual: Enhancing Self-Talk

This is an opportune time to focus on positive self-talk and reinforce your intention and goal. Use symbolic tools to enhance your commitment to constructive and affirming internal conversations.

You Need:

- A physical representation of your intention (e.g., a written note, a symbolic item).
- A white candle to symbolize clarity of thought.
- An item to represent air (such as feathers, incense, or a bell), symbolizing Gemini's airy nature.
- An item to represent the throat chakra, like a blue crystal or scarf, to enhance communication energy.

To Begin:

- Arrange your tools on your altar or in your sacred space. If you feel called to do so, cast a circle to create a protected and sacred environment for your ritual.

The Ritual:

- Light your white candle, focusing on the intention of clear and positive self-communication.
- Sit comfortably with your eyes closed, facing your altar.

- Hold the physical representation of your intention in your hands or keep it close to you.
- Visualize your intention radiating throughout your body. See your throat chakra glowing with a brilliant blue light, enhancing your ability to communicate positively with yourself.
- Out loud, or by writing on a piece of paper, affirm your commitment to positive self-talk. You can say or write, "With positive words I speak to myself, For my intention this wish I hold."
- Feel the power of your words reinforcing your intention and commitment.
- Choose one of your items (e.g., the air symbol or throat chakra item) to be a representation of your positive self-talk throughout this moon cycle.
- Hold it in your hand, allowing your intention and commitment to positive self-talk to flow through your body and into the item. Feel it becoming charged with your energy and purpose.
- Snuff out the candle, symbolizing the internalization of your intention and commitment.
- If you cast a circle, close it now, thanking any energies or entities you called upon for their guidance and protection.
- Keep the item you charged as a constant reminder of your commitment to positive self-talk. Place it somewhere you will see it often.

This Waxing Crescent Moon ritual in Gemini is a powerful way to harness the communicative energy of Gemini. By focusing on positive self-talk and reinforcing your intentions, you align yourself with Gemini's strengths in communication, setting a foundation for personal growth and fulfillment in the lunar cycle ahead.

GEMINI FIRST QUARTER MOON

Take Diverse Actions

GEMINI FIRST QUARTER MOON
QUICKIE
For the busiest of magical bees.

Busy Witch Ritual:

Engage in various activities related to your intention. Keep it light and fun, allowing for a mix of experiences.

Self-Care Tip:

Try a new hobby or activity that challenges your mind and keeps you agile.

Affirmation:

I embrace the dynamic energy of Gemini to confidently communicate my needs and take decisive steps towards my goals, balancing thought and action with ease and adaptability. I remember that there is a time for rest and a time for action. I am not held back right now as I create a reality that allows me to feel the way I want to feel.

Gemini First Quarter Moon Ritual: Action Planning

Gather information, communicate effectively, and strategize. Identify actionable steps, address unanswered questions, and prepare a solid plan to bring your intentions to fruition.

You Need:
- A journal or notebook and a pen for recording your thoughts and plans.
- A comfortable and quiet space where you can think, research, and plan without interruption.

To Begin:
- At the top of your paper, write down the intention you set during the New Moon. Keep it clear and concise.

The Ritual:
- Sit comfortably with your journal, taking a few deep breaths to center yourself.
- Reflect on your intention set during the New Moon.
- Begin to jot down questions related to your intention. Consider what first steps you can take today, what future actions are needed, any unanswered questions, the support you might need, past experiences with similar intentions, and potential barriers.

- Allow yourself to freely write down all thoughts and queries that surface, no matter how big or small.
- Use this time to do any necessary research. Look up information online, read relevant books or articles, or consult experts if needed.
- Aim to answer as many of your questions as possible, gathering the information that will help you move forward.
- Identify who in your network can provide support or guidance. Reach out to these individuals, whether for advice, encouragement, or practical help.
- With the information and support identified, start outlining a plan of action. Break down your intention into smaller, manageable steps.
- Write these steps in your journal, creating a clear roadmap towards achieving your intention.
- Close your journaling session with an affirmation of your commitment to your intention. You might say, "With clarity and purpose, I take actionable steps towards my intention, guided by the wisdom and communicative strength of Gemini."
- Begin to implement your action steps, using the momentum of the First Quarter Moon to propel you forward.
- Keep your journal handy to note progress, challenges, and insights as you work towards your intention.

This First Quarter Moon ritual in Gemini is a practical way to harness the communicative and intellectual energy of Gemini for practical action. By focusing on gathering information, seeking support, and creating a detailed plan, you align yourself with Gemini's strengths, setting a solid foundation for the realization of your intentions in the lunar cycle ahead.

GEMINI WAXING GIBBOUS MOON

Expand and Strategize

GEMINI
WAXING GIBBOUS MOON
QUICKIE
For the busiest of magical bees.

Busy Witch Ritual:

Watch the clouds and embrace how they shift and float as needed. Know that you can do the same.

Self-Care Tip:

Enjoy a playful exercise, like a puzzle or game, to keep your mind sharp and adaptable.

Affirmation:

As the Waxing Gibbous Moon brightens in Gemini, I trust in the power of my intellect and intuition, weaving together knowledge and insight to guide my path forward with clarity and purpose. I trust in the ever present duality of acting and receiving, shadow and light, as I pursue a life that supports the way I want to feel.

Gemini Waxing Gibbous Moon Ritual: Expand Knowledge

Explore various strategies, experiences, and insights from others who have pursued similar intentions. This ritual will help you enrich your understanding and refine your approach to your intention for this lunar cycle.

You Need:
- Access to research tools like books or the internet.
- A journal or notebook and a pen for taking notes.

To Begin:
- Choose a quiet and comfortable spot where you can read, listen, and reflect without distractions.
- Optionally, you can light a candle or incense to create a focused ambiance.

The Ritual:
- Begin by clearly stating your intention for this lunar cycle. Write it down in your journal.
- Reflect on what this intention means to you and why it's important.
- Immerse yourself in researching how others have achieved similar goals. Look for strategies, tools, and resources they used, challenges they faced, and how they overcame them.

- Explore various mediums — read books or blogs, watch vlogs, listen to podcasts. Absorb a range of perspectives and experiences.
- As you gather information, jot down key points, strategies, and ideas that resonate with you in your journal.
- Organize these insights in a way that makes sense to you — perhaps categorizing them by strategy, resource, or challenge.
- Take time to reflect on the information you've gathered. How can these insights be applied to your intention?
- Begin to formulate a plan or add to your existing plan. Incorporate the strategies and resources you've discovered that could be beneficial for your goal.
- Close your research session with an affirmation of your commitment to learning and applying these new insights. You might say, "With the knowledge I've gained, I am better equipped to realize my intention."
- Thank the energies of Gemini and the Waxing Gibbous Moon for their guidance and the wealth of information available to you.
- If you lit a candle or incense, safely extinguish it as you conclude your ritual.
- Implement the strategies and use the resources you've identified. Observe how they impact your progress towards your intention.

This Waxing Gibbous Moon ritual in Gemini is a practical way to deepen your understanding and refine your approach to achieving a goal. By embracing Gemini's love for knowledge and diverse experiences, you enrich your journey towards achieving your goals, equipped with a broader perspective and practical strategies.

GEMINI FULL MOON

Harvest and Appreciate

GEMINI FULL MOON
QUICKIE
For the busiest of magical bees.

Busy Witch Ritual:

Record yourself talking about yourself as the hero of your own story. Play it back and let it wash away self-doubt.

Self-Care Tip:

Have lunch or coffee with a friend to fill your cup!

Affirmation:

Under the luminous Gemini Full Moon, I embrace the duality within me, celebrating my versatility and adaptability, and confidently expressing my truth in all its forms. There is a shadow and light to every element of my journey and both are needed. I release inner resistance to feeling the way I want to feel.

Gemini Full Moon Ritual: Embrace Multiple Perspectives

Gemini's dual nature invites us to look at our intention and goals from new angles, whether they are manifesting as planned or revealing new paths and possibilities. Use the elements of air and sound to facilitate a reflective experience.

You Need:
- Incense, a humidifier, or a bowl of hot water for steam.
- Music that resonates with you and aids in reflection.
- A comfortable and quiet space where you can be undisturbed.

To Begin:
- Begin by playing your chosen music to set the tone for reflection.
- Light your incense, turn on your humidifier, or prepare your bowl of hot water to create a flow of air or vapor around you.

The Ritual:
- Sit comfortably and close your eyes, allowing yourself to become fully present in the moment.
- Take deep breaths, feeling the energy of the Full Moon and the air element around you.
- Reflect on your goal and intention set during the New Moon. Consider its progress, wins, and challenges. What lessons have you learned? Where can improvements be made?

- With Gemini's influence, allow your mind to explore multiple perspectives of your intention. Consider different outcomes, alternative paths, and the potential impact on yourself and others.
- If your intention has manifested, think about how you can build upon this success. What opportunities are emerging? How can you use Gemini's adaptability to take the next steps?
- If your intention hasn't fully come to fruition, ponder whether it has illuminated a different, perhaps more significant goal. Is it a stepping stone towards something else? How has it benefited you or those around you?
- Envision all your thoughts, reflections, and insights being absorbed by the smoke or vapor swirling around you.
- When you feel ready, open your eyes and gently blow the smoke or vapor away, symbolically releasing your intention into the universe.
- See this act as either a release of your intention, allowing it to transform or evolve, or as a prayer for the universe to bring you clarity and opportunities for action.
- Thank the energies of Gemini and the Full Moon for their illuminating and insightful influence.
- Allow the incense to burn out or turn off your humidifier. Sit for a few moments in gratitude for the clarity and perspectives gained.
- Use the revelations from this ritual to inform your actions and decisions in the next lunar cycle, embracing Gemini's flexibility and curiosity.

This Gemini Full Moon ritual is a wonderful way to engage with the reflective energy of the Full Moon, using Gemini's gift of perspective to gain deeper understanding and clarity about your intention and path forward. By embracing the air element and the power of reflection, you open yourself to new possibilities and directions.

GEMINI WANING GIBBOUS MOON

Bask in Knowledge

GEMINI
WANING GIBBOUS MOON
QUICKIE
For the busiest of magical bees.

Busy Witch Ritual:

Impart the knowledge and insights gained and speak your experience aloud for the universe to hear. Imagine your past self receiving the information and feeling safe and healed, knowing you're okay.

Self-Care Tip:

Explore a variety of perspectives on one topic to stretch your mind and fuel your confidence cup.

Affirmation:

As the Gemini moon wanes, I embrace the power of adaptability and communication, letting go of uncertainty and welcoming clarity and connection in my life. I give back to myself and the collective with the optimistic and positive words I speak. I allow myself to feel the way I want to feel.

Gemini Waning Gibbous Moon Ritual: Self-Gratitude

Gemini's communicative energy emphasizes the importance of acknowledging and appreciating the journey, not just the destination. Writing a thank you card to yourself serves as a powerful reminder of your dedication, struggles, and the positive changes you've made.

You Need:

- A beautiful thank you card or a piece of stationery and a pen.
- An envelope to seal your message.
- A quiet and comfortable space for reflection and writing.

To Begin:

- Before writing, take a moment to reflect on the journey towards your goal and intention. Think about the struggles you've faced, the changes you've made in your thought patterns or daily activities, and the vision you have for your future once your intention is realized.

The Ritual:

- Address the card to yourself, acknowledging your efforts, dedication, and the sacrifices you've made.
- Express gratitude for each step you've taken, no matter how small. Recognize the growth and learning that have occurred along the way.
- Write about how realizing this intention will make you feel and the positive impact it will have on your life.

- Once you've finished writing, place the thank you card in the envelope as a symbolic gesture of preserving your words of gratitude and acknowledgment.
- On the front of the envelope, you might write a message to yourself like, "Open when you need a reminder of your strength and dedication."
- Hold the sealed envelope in your hands for a few moments. Close your eyes and take deep breaths, feeling a sense of accomplishment and self-appreciation.
- Visualize yourself opening this envelope in the future, at a moment when you might need encouragement or a reminder of your journey.
- Place the envelope in a special or visible spot where you can easily access it when needed.
- Thank the energies of Gemini and the Disseminating Moon for their guidance and the ability to communicate and express gratitude.

This Disseminating Moon ritual in Gemini is a meaningful way to connect with yourself and recognize the efforts you've put into manifesting your goal and intention. By writing a thank you card to yourself, you not only celebrate your progress but also create a lasting reminder of your resilience and dedication.

GEMINI THIRD QUARTER MOON
Release and Reorganize

GEMINI THIRD QUARTER MOON
QUICKIE
For the busiest of magical bees.

Busy Witch Ritual:

Let go of what hasn't served you. Hold a candle in your hand and envision all thoughts and conversations that aren't nurturing leaving your energy. Light the candle and extinguish it when you're ready to let go.

Self-Care Tip:

Do a digital detox or organize your workspace to clear your mind. Reorganize your approach to something that feels sticky to be more effective.

Affirmation:

Under the Gemini Third Quarter Moon, I release indecision and embrace the wisdom of duality, finding balance and insight in every choice I make. I think in new ways about my life and explore new possibilities available to me as I continue to create an inner energy that allows me to feel the way I want to feel.

Gemini Third Quarter Moon Ritual: Expand Knowledge and Nurture Relationships

♊

Gemini's intellectual curiosity and association with The Lovers tarot card provide a perfect backdrop for deepening knowledge and understanding in various aspects of life, especially in relationships.

You Need:
- Choose a subject or area that interests you and aligns with your intention or goal for the next moon cycle. It could be a skill, a hobby, or deeper knowledge about a specific topic.
- If you use tarot cards, prepare them for a spread focusing on Focus, Choice, and Communication.

To Begin:
- Think about the relationships in your life that you'd like to strengthen or where communication can be improved.
- Dedicate time to learn something new or dive deeper into your chosen topic. This could involve reading, taking an online course, or engaging in a practical learning experience.
- As you learn, think about how this new knowledge can be applied in the next moon cycle and how it builds upon the lessons learned in the current cycle.

The Ritual:

- Take time to show appreciation in your relationships. Communicate your gratitude and affection to friends, family, or colleagues.
- Reflect on what each person brings to the relationship and acknowledge the beauty and growth in these connections.
- If you use tarot cards, do a spread focusing on Focus, Choice, and Communication. Ask where to focus your energy, the choices available to you, and where communication needs to be enhanced or initiated.
- Reflect on the messages from the cards and how they can guide your actions in the coming cycle.
- As the Third Quarter Moon is a time for release, consciously let go of any unused energy. Do this with a sense of joy and gratitude for the experiences and lessons of the past cycle.
- Close your ritual by thanking the energies of Gemini and the moon for their guidance and insights.
- Let this new understanding inform your decisions and actions as you transition into the next lunar cycle.

By engaging in learning, conversation, and tarot reflection, you not only release unused energy but also prepare yourself for the next moon cycle with a deeper understanding and strengthened relationships.

GEMINI WANING CRESCENT MOON
Rest and Reflect

GEMINI
WANING CRESCENT MOON
QUICKIE
For the busiest of magical bees.

Busy Witch Ritual:

Slow down and reflect on your journey. Think about what you've learned and how it has enriched your life. Light a candle and blow it out with a wish like you would a birthday candle.

Self-Care Tip:

Enjoy a quiet evening with a book or podcast that stimulates your mind and soothes your soul.

Affirmation:

As the Gemini Waning Crescent Moon fades, I trust in the power of communication and adaptability, ready to welcome new beginnings with an open mind and heart. I rest and receive, reflect and reset.

Gemini Waning Crescent Moon Ritual: Breathwork and Visualization

Gemini's association with the air element and the eastern coordinate point enhances a breathwork practice, making it an ideal time for mental clarity, reflection, and emotional release.

You Need:
- Choose a piece of music featuring wind instruments that you find relaxing and conducive to reflection.
- Find a quiet, comfortable place where you can sit or lie down undisturbed. You may want to dim the lights or light a candle to create a calming atmosphere.
- Keep a journal and pen nearby to record any insights, emotions, or divine downloads that may arise during the ritual.

To Begin:
- Start playing your selected wind instrument music. Allow its soothing tones to fill your space, setting the stage for relaxation and introspection.
- Sit or lie down comfortably. Close your eyes and begin to focus on your breathing.

The Ritual:

- As you inhale, visualize yourself filling up with abundance and gratitude. Imagine these positive energies entering your body with each breath.
- As you exhale, visualize any negative energy, stress, or unwanted thoughts leaving your body. See them being carried away with each out-breath.
- Continue this breathing pattern for the duration of the song or as long as you feel comfortable.
- With each breath, deepen your sense of relaxation and release. Feel yourself becoming lighter and more at peace.
- After completing your breathwork and visualization, take some time to sit quietly and absorb the experience.
- Open your journal and write down any significant feelings, thoughts, or 'divine downloads' that came to you during the exercise. Note any emotional experiences or insights that felt particularly meaningful.
- Gently bring your awareness back to your surroundings. Take a few deep breaths to ground yourself.
- Express gratitude for the insights and release you experienced during the ritual.
- If you used a candle, safely extinguish it as a symbolic end to your session.

By engaging with the air element inherent in Gemini, you create space for new beginnings and prepare yourself to embrace the opportunities of the upcoming lunar cycle with a clear mind and a rejuvenated spirit.

GEMINI RITUAL NOTES

GEMINI RITUAL NOTES

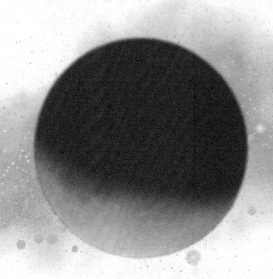

CANCER

Cancer, the fourth sign of the zodiac, is a symbol of emotional depth, nurturing, and intuitive understanding. Connect deeply with your feelings, care for yourself and others, and find comfort in the familiar. When the Moon is in Cancer, turn inward to listen to your heart, and to nurture your emotional well-being,.

Cancer energy is both soothing and emotionally disruptive. Let's look at its complexities – sometimes the protective nature of Cancer can lead to over-sensitivity or defensiveness, making it hard to step out of your comfort zone or release emotional baggage (even the most caring nurturers can find it tough to let go of old hurts).

Just as Cancer energy can offer emotional security, it can also lead to a tendency to cling to the past. What begins as a healthy attachment to loved ones or cherished memories can sometimes evolve into an inability to embrace change or new opportunities. Cancer's energy teaches us the importance of emotional resilience – the ability to care deeply while also allowing ourselves to grow, adapt, and welcome new experiences.

Cancer Moon Toolkit

Here are some suggested tools for your Cancer moon ritual kit. Keep in mind that everything is optional and the only true requirement is your energy, magic, and belief!

🌙 **Sun Sign Dates:** June 21-July 22

🌙 **Candle Color:** Silver

🌙 **Oil or Essence:** Chamomile (for nurturing and comfort)

🌙 **Herb:** Moonwort (for intuition and protection)

🌙 **Spell Focus:** Emotional depth and home

🌙 **Element:** Water   🌙 **Tarot:** Cups

🌙 **Crystal:** Moonstone

🌙 **Mythology:** The Crab, Hera, and Heracles

Cancer in My Chart

Refer to your birth chart and look for Cancer. It may be marked with this symbol: ♋

🌙 **House(s):**

🌙 **Planet(s):**

🌙 **Notes:**

Whenever the Moon is in Cancer, it will highlight this part of your birth chart and you may notice heightened emotions in this area or shadow aspects of your life or energy coming to the surface.

CANCER
NEW MOON
Set Intention with Care

CANCER NEW MOON
QUICKIE
For the busiest of magical bees.

Busy Witch Ritual:

In a quiet, cozy spot, set an intention that nurtures your emotional well-being or family life.

Self-Care Tip:

Try a comforting ritual, like lighting a candle or wrapping yourself in a soft blanket, to enhance the feeling of emotional security.

Affirmation:

Under the nurturing Cancer New Moon, I embrace emotional healing and the comfort of home, setting intentions that cultivate love, security, and deep inner peace. I hold the way I want to feel in my heart and carry it with me as I move into the lunar cycle.

Cancer New Moon Ritual: Creating a Home Sanctuary

Cancer's connection to the home and family makes this an ideal time to create a space that supports emotional well-being and relaxation. Cleanse your space, create a cozy area, and use tools like crystals or candles to amplify nurturing energy.

You Need:

- A tool for cleansing your space.
- A crystal or candle to amplify energy.
- Salt for protection and purification.
- Comfortable and cozy items to enhance your chosen area (like cushions, blankets, or a favorite book).
- Select an area in your home that you wish to transform into a nurturing sanctuary where you can relax, read, and enjoy peaceful moments .

To Begin:

- Begin by spiritually cleansing your living space with your chosen tool. As you do this, visualize any negative energy being cleared away, leaving a calm and positive atmosphere.
- Tidy up and arrange your chosen area. Make it feel extra cozy and welcoming with comfortable items that bring you joy and relaxation.

The Ritual:

- Set up your crystal or candle in this space as a focal point for nurturing energy.

- Walk around the outside of your home clockwise, sprinkling salt with the intention of keeping positive energy in and negative energy out.
- If you live in an apartment or prefer not to use salt outside, place a small amount of salt in containers at entryways as a symbol of protection.
- Sit in your newly arranged space with your crystal or candle.
- Visualize nurturing, welcoming energy spreading throughout your home.
- Speak the following affirmation out loud three times: "I live in a peaceful and loving home, I feel welcome and warm in my home, I am able to relax and be at ease in my home."
- Conclude with a statement of affirmation, such as "And so it is," to seal the energy.
- Spend some time in your cozy space, allowing yourself to fully absorb and amplify the nurturing energy. Whether it's through reading, meditating, or simply sitting in stillness, let this be a moment of peace and comfort.
- Return to this space whenever you need to recharge or seek comfort. It's now a sanctuary infused with the nurturing energy of Cancer and the New Moon.
- Maintain the cleanliness and coziness of this area to continually support your emotional well-being.

By focusing on creating a space of comfort and relaxation, you align with Cancer's emphasis on home and emotional well-being, fostering a sense of peace and serenity that you can return to throughout the lunar cycle.

CANCER WAXING CRESCENT MOON
Cultivate Emotional Roots

CANCER
WAXING CRESCENT MOON
QUICKIE
For the busiest of magical bees.

Busy Witch Ritual:

Reflect on how your daily routines can nurture your intention. Incorporate small acts of self-care and emotional nourishment as a ritual to settle into your intention.

Self-Care Tip:

Cooking a family recipe or a meal that brings back fond memories.

Affirmation:

As the Cancer Moon waxes, I gently nurture my intentions, allowing them to grow with care and compassion, just like the protective embrace of a loving home. I carry nurturing energy with me as I grow, explore, and learn this lunar cycle.

Cancer Waxing Crescent Moon Ritual: Soothing Bath

Cancer's lunar water energy is perfectly suited for a relaxing and releasing bath, allowing you to honor your emotions and wash away anything that does not align with how you want to feel.

You Need:
- A few candles to set the scene.
- Crystals like Angelite and Moonstone.
- Your favorite calming music.
- 1 cup of sea salt or Epsom salt for purification and relaxation.
- 1 cup of apple cider vinegar to cleanse and rejuvenate your skin and spirit.
- Scented herbs like lavender to add to the bath if you desire.

To Begin:
- Arrange your crystals and candles in the bathroom to set the mood and turn on the music.
- Draw a warm bath, adding the sea salt or Epsom salt, apple cider vinegar, and the herbs. Stir the water gently to mix the ingredients.

The Ritual:
- Ease yourself into the bath, feeling the warm embrace of the water.

- Close your eyes and take deep, slow breaths, allowing yourself to fully relax and be present in this nurturing moment.
- Meditate on the events and emotions of this moon cycle. What has served its purpose? What can you release? Visualize these elements washing away from you, dissolving in the water.
- As you soak, imagine all that you wish to release being drawn out by the salt and the soothing oils. Envision these energies going down the drain at the end of your bath.
- Take as much time as you need in this reflective state. This is your time for healing and emotional care.
- When you feel ready, slowly rise from the bath. As you drain the water, visualize all that you've released flowing away, leaving you cleansed and rejuvenated.
- Blow out the candles, thanking the nurturing energies of Cancer and the Waxing Crescent Moon for their support.
- Continue to nurture yourself throughout the lunar cycle. Remember the feelings of calm and release from your bath whenever you need emotional comfort.
- Keep the Angelite and Moonstone close by, perhaps on your nightstand or in a place where you often relax, to maintain the connection to the nurturing energy you cultivated.
- Reflect on your emotional journey in a journal, noting how the ritual bath aided in your emotional release and self-care.

This Waxing Crescent Moon ritual in Cancer is a deeply soothing and nurturing practice, aligning with Cancer's emphasis on emotional care and comfort. By creating a sacred space for relaxation and reflection, you honor your emotional needs and set a tone of self-care and rejuvenation for the lunar cycle ahead.

CANCER FIRST QUARTER MOON

Build Emotional Strength

CANCER FIRST QUARTER MOON
QUICKIE
For the busiest of magical bees.

Busy Witch Ritual:

Focus on building emotional resilience related to your intention. Address any emotional barriers with compassion. Jot them down and get them out of your head. Throw the paper away or burn it.

Self-Care Tip:

Take a warm bath or enjoy a soothing skincare routine to nurture your body and soul before or after taking action under the Cancer First Quarter Moon.

Affirmation:

Under this Cancer First Quarter Moon, I embrace the strength of my emotions, channeling them into decisive actions that align with my deepest needs and nurture my soul's journey. My emotional well is deep and wide with each feeling and experience serving a purpose. I take action to feel the way I want to feel.

Cancer First Quarter Moon Ritual: Emotional Alignment

Create a sacred space that aligns your emotional self with how you want to feel, helping to overcome doubts and reinforce positive feelings. This ritual aids in manifesting your intention and goal with emotional power.

You Need:
- A mirror or mirror plate to reflect and amplify your intention and goal.
- A white candle for purity, clarity, and focus.
- Crystals that resonate with the emotions you wish to enhance (e.g., Rose Quartz for love, Citrine for confidence or creativity, Red Jasper for safety or steadfastness).

To Begin:
- Place the mirror or mirror plate in your chosen spot.
- Arrange the white candle and your selected crystals on the mirror. The reflective surface will help to amplify the energy of the items.

The Ritual:
- Light the white candle, focusing on its flame as a symbol of the clarity and emotional aspect of your intention and goal.
- Hold each crystal in your hand, one at a time, and connect with its energy. Feel its emotional resonance within you.

- As you hold each crystal, state an affirmation out loud, such as "I am surrounded by love," "I am filled with confidence," or "I am steadfast and secure." Repeat this affirmation as many times as you feel necessary, allowing the emotion to fill you.
- Place the crystals back on the mirror around the candle.
- Sit or stand in front of your sacred space, taking a few deep breaths. Feel the alignment of your emotional self with your intention.
- Visualize your intention coming to fruition, supported by the emotional energy you've cultivated.
- Leave your sacred space set up throughout the First Quarter Moon phase. Return to it whenever you need to realign your emotions with your intention and goal.
- Each time you visit your space, repeat your affirmations, reinforcing the emotional connection to your goal.
- When you feel your emotional energy is fully aligned with your intention, gently blow out the candle, thanking the energies of Cancer and the First Quarter Moon for their support.
- Keep the space intact as a reminder of your emotional power and intention. Dismantle it with gratitude after three days or whenever you feel ready.
- As the moon cycle progresses, observe how the emotional energy you've harnessed influences your actions and brings you closer to your goals.

This First Quarter Moon ritual in Cancer is a nurturing and empowering practice, aligning your emotional energy with your intention and goal. By creating a sacred space dedicated to your emotional body, you strengthen your resolve and move forward with confidence and clarity, supported by the nurturing energy of Cancer.

CANCER WAXING GIBBOUS MOON
Refine and Fulfill

CANCER
WAXING GIBBOUS MOON
QUICKIE
For the busiest of magical bees.

Busy Witch Ritual:

Review your emotional journey. Connect deeper with your intention and make any necessary adjustments. Hold a cup of tea or a glass of water and imagine being supported emotionally by the universe as you drink it.

Self-Care Tip:

A heart-to-heart conversation with a loved one or journaling to explore your inner world.

Affirmation:

As the Cancer Waxing Gibbous Moon illuminates my path, I trust in the flow of my intuition, nurturing my dreams and cultivating resilience with each step forward. The universe supports me fully as long as I'm supporting myself. I trust that I have what it takes to feel the way I want to feel.

Cancer Waxing Gibbous Moon Ritual: Fulfillment

Cancer's nurturing and intuitive energy provides the perfect backdrop for a deep, heart-to-heart conversation with yourself, cleansing your energy and preparing for the culmination of your intention.

You Need:
- Choose soothing and uplifting music that resonates with your soul.
- Gather any bath products that make you feel luxurious.

To Begin:
- Think about what you want to do for the full moon and gather your altar supplies.

The Ritual:
- Begin your shower, letting the warm water cascade over you. Close your eyes and take deep, calming breaths.
- Envision the water not just cleansing your body, but also your mind and spirit. Imagine it washing away any residual energy from actions not taken, leaving you with a focused and clean slate.
- Concentrate on the actions you have taken towards your intention. Acknowledge and nurture these steps, feeling proud and trusting in their alignment with your goals.

- As you shower, affirm your trust in yourself and the universe. You might say, "I trust in my actions and my path. I nurture my intention with love and confidence."
- Feel the water element of Cancer soothing and cleansing you, preparing you for the revelations of the Full Moon.
- After your shower, begin to prepare for the Full Moon.
- Create a space for your Full Moon ritual, selecting items that resonate with your intention and make you feel empowered.
- Reflect on the beauty of both the challenges and successes you've encountered. Acknowledge that there is learning and growth in every experience.
- Prepare yourself mentally and emotionally for whatever the Full Moon may bring, knowing that you are ready to embrace it all.
- In the days leading up to the Full Moon, continue to nurture yourself and your intention. Keep your energy focused and aligned with your goal.
- Revisit your plans for the Full Moon ritual, ensuring that everything is set to create a magical and empowering experience.
- Carry the sense of trust, nurture, and preparation with you, letting it infuse your actions and thoughts as you move closer to the culmination of your intentions.

This Waxing Gibbous Moon ritual is a deeply nurturing and preparatory practice, aligning your emotional and spiritual self with the forthcoming Full Moon. By cleansing your energy and preparing yourself both inside and out, you honor the nurturing essence of Cancer, ready to embrace the fulfillment and revelations of your intention.

CANCER FULL MOON

Celebrate Self Appreciation

CANCER FULL MOON
QUICKIE
For the busiest of magical bees.

Busy Witch Ritual:

Write one sentence that makes you feel emotionally alive and carry that energy with you over the next few days.

Self-Care Tip:

Creating a small, intimate celebration at home, like a candlelit dinner or a movie night. Go solo or invite friends or family!

Affirmation:

Under the luminous Cancer Full Moon, I embrace my emotional strength, celebrate my growth, and honor the deep connections that enrich my life. I go within when I need to and explore new horizons when I need to. I carry the tools to feel the way I want to feel within me.

Cancer Full Moon Ritual: Nurturing Self-Appreciation Bath

This ritual for the Cancer Full Moon is designed to foster self-appreciation, gratitude, and nurturing. Cancer's connection to emotional depth and comfort makes a special bath ritual the perfect way to honor yourself, reflect on your achievements, and celebrate your unique qualities.

You Need:

- Epsom salts or sea salt for cleansing and relaxation.
- Your favorite herbs or bath addition for aromatic pleasure and emotional upliftment.
- Flower petals to add beauty and a touch of nature.
- A candle for a soft, soothing light.
- Your favorite drink, be it tea, cocoa, a fruit juice blend, or a smoothie, to hydrate and indulge.
- Soft, gentle music to create a serene atmosphere.
- A nice, soft towel for comfort.

To Begin:

- Choose a time when you won't be disturbed. Set up your bathroom to be a haven of relaxation. Arrange everything you need within easy reach.
- Draw a warm bath, adding the Epsom or sea salt, your favorite bath aromatic, and the flower petals if you're using them.

- Start your music and light the candle to enhance the calming ambiance.
- Ease into the bath, allowing yourself to fully relax and immerse in the nurturing environment.
- Sip on your chosen drink, letting its warmth or freshness complement the soothing water.
- Reflect on your intention set during the New Moon. Acknowledge all your achievements and progress made in the last two weeks.
- Think about the aspects of your life that bring you joy and for which you are grateful.
- Turn your thoughts inward, focusing on your strengths, talents, and what makes you uniquely wonderful.
- Contemplate any self-limiting beliefs or stories you tell yourself. Recognize them and gently let them go, affirming your worth and potential.
- After your bath, while wrapped in your soft towel, take some time to journal your reflections. Keep the candle lit and the music playing to maintain the mood and energy.
- Write about your achievements, the things you're grateful for, your strengths, and any insights about self-imposed limitations.
- Once you've finished journaling, blow out the candle, thanking the Cancer Full Moon for its illuminating energy and the opportunity for deep emotional reflection.

By taking the time to nurture yourself in a soothing bath, you honor the nurturing essence of Cancer, allowing for deep emotional healing and self-appreciation. This ritual sets a tone of loving kindness and gratitude, empowering you to embrace your full potential.

CANCER WANING GIBBOUS MOON

Gratitude and Release

CANCER
WANING GIBBOUS MOON
QUICKIE
For the busiest of magical bees.

Busy Witch Ritual:

Hold your favorite body lotion or oil in your hands and say loving words to yourself before applying.

Self-Care Tip:

Practice relational self-care and nurture someone in your life to create and strengthen connection.

Affirmation:

As the Cancer Moon wanes, I release emotional burdens with grace, trusting the ebb and flow of life to guide me towards inner peace and healing. When I feel the way I want to feel, I have greater capacity for others and can easily spread magic throughout the universe.

Cancer Waning Gibbous Moon Ritual: Water Gratitude

Embrace the ebb and flow of life through a gratitude practice by a natural water source. Cancer's deep connection to water and the moon's influence on the tides make this an ideal setting for acknowledging life's highs and lows and finding gratitude in all experiences.

You Need:
- Choose a location near an ocean, lake, river, or any natural body of water where you can safely and comfortably perform the ritual.

To Begin:
- Before heading to the water, take a moment to reflect on the recent experiences in your life. Think about both the positive and challenging moments.

The Ritual:
- Once you arrive at the water, take a few moments to connect with the environment. Feel the breeze, listen to the sound of the water, and observe its movements.
- Stand, sit, or walk along the edge of the water, allowing yourself to be present in this natural setting.
- Reflect on the high points in your life, feeling gratitude for the joy, growth, and blessings they've brought.

- Then, consider the low points. Acknowledge the lessons learned or the strength gained from these challenges.
- You can write these reflections down, say them out loud, or simply think about them, whatever feels most natural to you.
- When you're ready, approach the water. Gently place your hands or feet in it, visualizing the water washing away any lingering negativity or pain from the challenging experiences.
- As you do this, imagine the water's flow taking away these remnants, leaving you cleansed and rejuvenated.
- Stand up and, if visible, raise your arms towards the moon. Thank the universe, spirit, or source for the good times and the abundance in your life.
- Feel the energy of the moon fueling your soul, filling you with gratitude and peace.
- Allow yourself to fully experience the range of emotions that come with this ritual. It's okay to feel both the highs and the lows.
- Acknowledge that every experience, whether joyful or challenging, is a part of your journey and contributes to your growth.
- Take a few more moments to bask in the tranquility of the water and the moonlight.
- When you feel complete, gently withdraw from the water and take a few deep breaths, grounding yourself.
- Thank the energies of Cancer and the Disseminating Moon for their guidance and the healing power of water.

By acknowledging and releasing the highs and lows of life in a natural setting, you embrace the full spectrum of your experiences, finding gratitude and healing in the rhythm of nature.

CANCER THIRD QUARTER MOON

Spread Kindness

CANCER THIRD QUARTER MOON

QUICKIE

For the busiest of magical bees.

Busy Witch Ritual:

Let go of any emotional baggage that's hindering your growth. Focus on healing and releasing past hurts. Jot down anything that's bothering you and throw it away.

Self-Care Tip:

Do a cleansing ritual, like energetically clearing your space or a gentle yoga session to release tension.

Affirmation:

Under this Cancer Third Quarter Moon, I embrace reflection and release, nurturing my soul and finding balance in letting go of what no longer serves my growth and well-being. I dream of my ideal future and carry that dream with me knowing a life that feels like magic begins with me.

Cancer Third Quarter Moon Ritual: Spreading Kindness

♋

Cancer's nurturing energy is perfect for giving back and raising the collective vibration through heartfelt gestures. This ritual combines the emotional depth of Cancer with the magic of giving.

You Need:
- Decide on a random act of kindness that resonates with you. It could be baking cookies with a magical sigil, creating a happiness charm, bringing flowers to someone, or assembling a magical tea basket.
- Collect the necessary items for your chosen act of kindness. This might include baking ingredients, herbs and oils for a charm, flowers, or tea and relaxation items for a basket.

To Begin:
- As you prepare your act of kindness, focus on infusing it with positive, nurturing energy. Visualize the joy and comfort it will bring to the recipient.

The Ritual:
- Engage in the preparation of your chosen act of kindness. If you're baking, focus on each step, infusing the cookies with love and positive intentions. If creating a charm or tea basket, select each item thoughtfully, charging them with calming and happy energy.

- As you prepare your offering, consider adding a magical element. This could be a sigil for happiness, a blessing for peace, or a charm for relaxation.
- If you're artistically inclined, you might also decorate your offering or its packaging with symbols or colors that represent nurturing and kindness.
- Once your offering is ready, go out and perform your act of kindness. This could be delivering your baked goods to neighbors, scattering your happiness charm in a community park, presenting flowers to someone, or giving the tea basket to a friend.
- As you do so, maintain a mindset of unconditional giving and openness. Feel the joy of contributing to someone else's happiness.
- After completing your act of kindness, take some time to reflect on the experience. How did it make you feel? What reactions did you observe?
- Consider journaling about the experience, focusing on the emotions it brought up and the connections it fostered.

This Third Quarter Moon ritual in Cancer is a beautiful way to harness the nurturing energy of the sign to spread joy and kindness. By stepping out of your comfort zone and engaging in acts of giving, you not only uplift others but also reinforce your own sense of purpose and connection to the universal energy of love and compassion.

CANCER WANING CRESCENT MOON

Rest and Go Inward

CANCER
WANING CRESCENT MOON
QUICKIE
For the busiest of magical bees.

Busy Witch Ritual:

Take time to rest and go inward. Reflect on your emotional journey and how it has shaped you. Listen to some meditative or calming music and let your spirit relax.

Self-Care Tip:

Enjoy a quiet evening with a comforting activity, like knitting or reading a favorite book.

Affirmation:

As the Cancer Waning Crescent Moon fades, I trust in the natural flow of life, releasing old emotions and patterns with grace, and preparing my heart for new beginnings with hope and serenity. I carry my future vision, intention, and goal with me always and am open to the ebbs and flows of the journey.

Cancer Waning Crescent Moon Ritual: Release and Renewal

This ritual is designed to help you reflect, rest, and release negative emotions. Cancer's deep emotional energy provides a supportive backdrop for letting go of what no longer serves you and embracing a more positive emotional state.

You Need:

- You might want to include comforting items like cushions, blankets, or anything that helps you feel relaxed and secure.
- Choose an issue or situation that is currently causing you negative emotions. Find and print out an image that represents these negative feelings for you. Then, find and print an image that symbolizes how you want to feel about this situation – something that represents positivity and healing.
- You'll need a safe way to burn the negative image, like a fireproof bowl or an outdoor fire pit.
- If you choose to bury the positive image, have a small shovel or trowel ready, along with a plant or a spot near a tree where you can bury it.

To Begin:

- Set up a space where you feel safe and at peace. This could be a corner of your room, a spot in your garden, or any place that feels sacred to you.

The Ritual:

- Sit quietly in your sacred space, holding the image that represents your negative emotions.
- Reflect on these feelings and acknowledge their presence in your life.
- When you're ready, safely burn the image. As it turns to ash, visualize the negative emotions being released and transmuted by the universe.
- Now, take the image that represents how you want to feel.
- Bury it in a plant pot or at the base of a tree. As you do this, imagine planting seeds of positive emotions and intentions.
- Visualize these positive feelings growing and blossoming around you, replacing the old, negative emotions.
- After completing the ritual, do something nurturing for yourself. This could be taking a nap, reading a book, having a cup of tea, or any activity that allows you to rest and rejuvenate.
- Allow yourself to relax fully, releasing any residual negative energy and embracing the new, positive emotional state.
- In the days following the ritual, take time to notice any shifts in your emotional state. Be mindful of how the release of negative emotions impacts your daily life.
- Tend to the plant or visit the tree where you buried the positive image, as a reminder of your commitment to nurturing positive emotions.

This ritual is a powerful way to engage with the moon's energy for emotional healing and renewal. By consciously releasing negative emotions and planting the seeds of positivity, you align with Cancer's nurturing essence, paving the way for emotional growth and inner peace.

CANCER RITUAL NOTES

CANCER RITUAL NOTES

LEO

Leo, the fifth sign of the zodiac, radiates with confidence, creativity, and a majestic sense of self. Embrace your inner strength, express yourself boldly, and step into the spotlight with courage. Tap into your personal power to showcase your talents and to pursue your passions with a fiery determination.

Leo energy is both inspiring and charismatic. However, it's essential to be mindful of its intensity – sometimes the lion-hearted nature of Leo can lead to ego-driven actions or a need for constant validation, making it challenging to recognize the value of humility or to appreciate the contributions of others.

Just as Leo energy can ignite a powerful sense of self-expression and leadership, it can also lead to a sense of overbearing pride. What starts as a healthy self-esteem and pursuit of one's goals can sometimes turn into an overwhelming desire for recognition and applause. Balance self-confidence with compassion and understanding that true leadership involves not just shining on our own, but also helping others to shine.

Leo Moon Toolkit

Here are some suggested tools for your Leo moon ritual kit. Keep in mind that everything is optional and the only true requirement is your energy, magic, and belief!

🌙 **Sun Sign Dates:** July 23-August 22

🌙 **Candle Color:** Gold

🌙 **Oil or Essence:** Frankincense (for confidence and warmth)

🌙 **Herb:** Sunflower (for vitality and leadership)

🌙 **Spell Focus:** Creativity and self-expression

🌙 **Element:** Fire   🌙 **Tarot:** Wands

🌙 **Crystal:** Citrine

🌙 **Mythology:** The Nemean Lion

Leo in My Chart

Refer to your birth chart and look for Leo. It may be marked with this symbol: ♌

🌙 **House(s):**

🌙 **Planet(s):**

🌙 **Notes:**

Whenever the Moon is in Leo, it will highlight this part of your birth chart and you may notice heightened emotions in this area or shadow aspects of your life or energy coming to the surface.

LEO
NEW MOON
Set Intention with Flair

LEO NEW MOON
QUICKIE
For the busiest of magical bees

Busy Witch Ritual:

Find a moment of solitude to set a bold, creative intention. Think about how this intention can bring more joy and self-expression into your life. Say it (or roar it) out loud!

Self-Care Tip:

Enjoy a quick, fun activity that sparks joy, like dancing to your favorite song or trying out a new makeup look.

Affirmation:

Under the New Moon in Leo, I embrace my inner strength and creativity, setting intentions that ignite my passion and confidence, shining brightly in my authentic truth. I take up space and shine my light with authenticity so I am free to feel the way I want to feel.

Leo New Moon
Ritual: Detox Bath

♌

Harness the fiery energy of Leo in a balanced way. The detox bath ritual helps to calm and center your energy, creating an ideal space for setting and feeling your intentions. Release negative energies and focus on what you wish to manifest.

You Need:
- 1/2 Tbsp dead sea salt and 1/2 Tbsp Himalayan salt for purification and grounding.
- A mix of dried herbs: 1/4 Tbsp each of calendula flowers, lavender flowers, lemon balm, rose petals, and jasmine flowers for relaxation and emotional balance.
- Choose crystals like Selenite and Moonstone, and any others you feel drawn to, for their calming and intuitive properties.

To Begin:
- Mix all the salts and dried herbs in a jar and gently shake to combine.
- If possible, let the mixture sit overnight, allowing the ingredients to synergize.

The Ritual:
- Draw a warm bath, adding Epsom salts for additional detoxification and relaxation.
- Place your herbal blend in a mesh teabag or a cloth sachet and immerse it in the bathwater.

- Arrange your selected crystals around the bath to create a serene and energetically charged environment.
- Dim the lights or light candles to create a soothing ambiance.
- You may choose to play soft, calming music or enjoy the silence, whichever aids your focus and relaxation.
- Ease into the bath, allowing yourself to fully relax and immerse in the experience.
- Focus on your breathing, letting each inhale draw in positivity and each exhale release any negativity.
- Visualize your intention for the new lunar cycle. Imagine it taking shape and form as you soak in the nurturing waters.
- After your bath, while wrapped in a cozy towel, take some time to journal about your intention. Write down how you envision it manifesting and the steps you can take to achieve it.
- Once you've finished journaling, take a moment to thank the energies of Leo and the New Moon for their guidance and strength.
- Gently blow out any candles, feeling centered and aligned with your intention.
- Remember the sense of balance and focus achieved during the bath whenever you need to realign with your goals.

This New Moon in Leo ritual is a perfect blend of fiery energy and calming water, helping you to detoxify negative energies and set clear, focused intentions. By taking the time for a nurturing bath ritual, you honor the Leo energy in a way that supports your emotional and spiritual well-being, setting a strong foundation for the lunar cycle ahead.

LEO WAXING CRESCENT MOON
Infuse Creativity

LEO
WAXING CRESCENT MOON
QUICKIE
For the busiest of magical bees.

Busy Witch Ritual:

Use your morning routine to remind yourself of your creative power. Speak your intention out loud in front of a mirror.

Self-Care Tip:

Be bold and try something new with your hair or make-up.

Affirmation:

As the Waxing Crescent Moon glows in Leo, I nurture my intentions with courage and heart, allowing my creativity and self-expression to flourish and grow. I am brave, bold, and believe in myself always.

Leo Waxing Crescent Moon Ritual: Invoking Courage

♌

This ritual for the Waxing Crescent Moon in Leo is designed to connect you with the courage and confidence characteristic of Leo. It focuses on empowering your intentions with the boldness and determination needed to bring them to fruition.

You Need:
- Choose a candle or incense that represents courage to you. This could be based on scent, color, or personal association.
- Pick an item to serve as your courage charm. It should be something small enough to carry with you, like a stone, a piece of jewelry, or a keychain.

To Begin:
- Find a quiet space where you can perform your ritual without interruptions.
- Arrange your candle or incense and charm in this space, creating a mini altar that radiates boldness and strength.

The Ritual:
- Begin by lighting your chosen candle or incense, letting its fragrance and energy fill the space.
- As it burns, focus on its symbolism, drawing in the essence of courage and fearlessness.

- Take the charm in your dominant hand, the one you use to take action and make things happen.
- Close your eyes and visualize your intention. Imagine yourself successfully achieving it, embodying the strength and bravery of a lion.
- Slowly pass the charm through the smoke of the candle or incense.
- As you do this, recite the affirmation: "Courage I wish to tie in, as I invoke the energy of a lion. Under this Leo moon, I have no doubt my intention will be here soon."
- Feel the charm absorbing the energy of your words and the courage of Leo.
- Once you feel the charm is fully charged, extinguish the candle or incense safely.
- Keep the charm with you throughout the moon cycle. Whenever you need a boost of courage, hold it and remember the affirmation.
- Regularly touch or look at your charm as a reminder of the courage within you and the support of the Leo energy.
- If you face challenges or moments of doubt, use the charm to center yourself and recall the boldness and determination you infused into it.
- As the moon cycle progresses, observe how carrying the charm influences your confidence and ability to pursue your intentions.

This Waxing Crescent Moon ritual in Leo is a powerful way to harness the fiery, courageous energy of Leo. By creating and carrying a courage charm, you remind yourself of your inner strength and the bold spirit needed to make your intentions a reality. Let this ritual be a source of empowerment and confidence as you dance through the lunar cycle.

LEO FIRST QUARTER MOON

Take Center Stage

LEO FIRST QUARTER MOON
QUICKIE
For the busiest of magical bees.

Busy Witch Ritual:

Be bold and visible in your actions. Wear something that FEELS like the action you want to take. Let the adornment be the magic.

Self-Care Tip:

Celebrate whatever steps you've taken with a bit of flair. Maybe some flowers and confetti for yourself?

Affirmation:

Under the First Quarter Moon in Leo, I boldly take action towards my goals, embracing my inner strength and shining with confidence in every step I take. I live in alignment with how I want to feel and am excited to live authentically, shining my light on the world.

Leo First Quarter Moon Ritual: Lioness Tarot Spread

♌

Use a tarot spread to explore your authentic self and the actions needed to manifest your intentions. Leo's energy of courage and self-awareness, tempered with mindfulness of the ego, provides a powerful backdrop for this introspective act.

You Need:

- Have your tarot deck ready. If you have a particular affinity with a deck that resonates with Leo's energy, consider using that.
- You might want to light a candle or incense to create a focused and sacred atmosphere.

To Begin:

- Choose a quiet and comfortable area where you can lay out your tarot cards without disturbance.
- Begin by shuffling your tarot deck, focusing on your intention and goal for this lunar cycle.

The Ritual:

- Draw cards for each position in the Lioness Tarot Spread placing them in any way that feels right for you right now:

- Intention: Either choose a card that represents your intention or draw one intuitively.
- Ego: Draw a card that reveals what aspect of your ego might be hindering your intention.
- Beginning: Draw a card that suggests the first few steps to overcome these ego challenges.
- Bridge: Draw a card that represents the newfound courage you can harness to move forward.
- Ending: Draw a card to reflect whether this intention is still true to your authentic self.

- Take time to contemplate the meaning of each card. How do they speak to your current situation, your strengths, and the areas where you need to grow?
- Consider how the 'Ego' card is influencing your path and what the 'Beginning' card suggests as initial steps to overcome this.
- Reflect on the 'Bridge' card. How can you use the courage it represents to advance toward your goals?
- Look at the 'Ending' card. Does it affirm that your intention aligns with your true self, or does it suggest a need for reevaluation?
- Write down your thoughts and feelings about each card and what they reveal about your journey. This can be a valuable reference as you progress through the lunar cycle.
- Take action based on your new information.

The Lioness Tarot Spread, offers an opportunity for self-discovery and alignment. It encourages a deep dive into your emotional body, helping to illuminate the path towards how you want to feel and the authentic expression of your inner self.

LEO WAXING GIBBOUS MOON
Refine and Shine

LEO
WAXING GIBBOUS MOON
QUICKIE
For the busiest of magical bees.

Busy Witch Ritual:

Review your progress and make any necessary tweaks. Keep your intention bright and in the spotlight. Hold a lit candle in your hand and focus on your intention. Blow it out and release it to the universe.

Self-Care Tip:

Enjoy a pampering session, like a facial or a luxurious hair treatment, to feel radiant and confident.

Affirmation:

As the Waxing Gibbous Moon glows in Leo, I trust in my creative power and the journey ahead, knowing that each step brings me closer to manifesting my truest desires with courage and heart. I stand in my full potential and feel the way I want to feel.

Leo Waxing Gibbous Moon Ritual: Intention Weaving

♌

This ritual will harness Leo's love for creativity and the introspective energy of the Waxing Gibbous Moon. Through a meditative paper weaving activity, you can channel your focus, calm your mind, and reinforce your intention.

You Need:
- Paper in various colors.
- Glue, scissors, and optional paper edging scissors for decorative cuts.
- Glitter glue, puffy paint, stickers, beads, or other decorative materials to embellish your weave.

To Begin:
- Choose a quiet and comfortable area where you can engage in your paper weaving without distractions.
- You might want to light a candle or play soft, soothing music to enhance the calming atmosphere.

The Ritual:
- Cut a piece of paper into a large square, approximately 8 inches on each side.
- Fold the paper in half and cut evenly spaced slits, about 1 inch wide, leaving an inch uncut at the edge.
- Carefully unfold the paper to reveal the vertical slits.

- Cut strips of colored paper, 1 inch wide and 10 inches long, to weave across your base.
- Start weaving the colored strips through the slits in your base paper, alternating over and under.
- With each weave, focus on your intention. As you pass each strip through, breathe in confidence and positivity for your intention.
- Continue weaving, pushing each strip to the top and alternating the pattern. Be mindful of your breath and thoughts as you do this.
- If doubts or negative thoughts arise, use the rhythm of your weaving to breathe them out, replacing them with confidence and clarity.
- Once your paper is fully woven, glue down the edges to secure the strips.
- Embellish your weave with glitter glue, stickers, or beads, allowing your creativity to flow.
- Once your paper weave is complete, spend a few moments reflecting on your intention and the process of creating your weave.
- Acknowledge the calmness and focus you've cultivated through this creative process.
- Place your completed paper weave in a spot where you'll see it over the next three days, as a reminder of your intention and the mindful focus you've dedicated to it.
- Thank the energies of Leo and the Waxing Gibbous Moon for their guidance and inspiration.

By engaging in a meditative crafting activity, you channel Leo's fiery energy into a focused and calming practice, aligning your mind and spirit with your goals. As you move through the lunar cycle, let this creative ritual be a reminder of your inner strength, creativity, and the power of focused intention.

LEO
FULL MOON
Celebrate with Glamour

LEO FULL MOON
QUICKIE
For the busiest of magical bees.

Busy Witch Ritual:

Celebrate your achievements with a bit of glamor and fun. Fancy yourself up and dress in a wildly delightful outfit that reflects the work you've been doing.

Self-Care Tip:

Host a small party or a glamorous night out to celebrate your successes.

Affirmation:

Under the radiant Full Moon in Leo, I celebrate my unique strengths and achievements. I shine brightly, embracing my confidence and the joy of self-expression, fully aligned with my purpose. I am filled with the courage to release what needs to go to make space to feel the way I want to feel.

Leo Full Moon Ritual: Charging Creative Tools for Creation

♌

This ritual for the Full Moon in Leo focuses on harnessing the vibrant, creative energy of Leo to charge your tools with creativity and intention. Empower the instruments you use to manifest your goal and intention, infusing them with the bold and expressive energy of the Leo Full Moon.

You Need:
- Choose the tools that you associate with your intention and creativity. This could be anything from art supplies, divination tools, kitchen utensils, exercise equipment, to something as simple as your wallet, planner, or pen and paper.

To Begin:
- Identify a cozy place in your home where you feel comfortable for the ritual.

The Ritual:
- As the Full Moon rises, arrange your chosen tools in the spot where they will catch the moonlight.
- As you place each item, hold it for a moment and focus on your intention. Visualize the tool being charged with the radiant energy of the Leo Full Moon.

- Leave your tools in the energy of the moon overnight. Imagine the moon's rays infusing them with creative power and the bold spirit of Leo.
- If you like, you can sit with your tools for a while, meditating under the energy, and reinforcing your connection to your intention.
- While your tools are charging, affirm their newfound energy. You might say, "Under this Leo Full Moon, I charge these tools with creativity, strength, and the power to manifest my intentions."
- Spend some time thinking about the next steps you'll take with your newly charged tools. How will you use them to move forward on your intention?
- Consider writing down a plan or a set of actions that you'll take in the coming days.
- Before you go to bed, or the next morning, collect your tools. Hold each one and feel its charged energy.
- Thank the Leo Full Moon for its empowering influence and express gratitude for the creativity and strength it has bestowed upon your tools.
- Stay open to the creative inspiration that Leo brings. Allow yourself to be bold and expressive in your pursuits.

This Leo Full Moon ritual is one way to connect with your creative spirit and empower the tools that aid in manifesting your intentions. By charging them under the Leo Full Moon, you infuse them with the energy needed to take bold action and bring your dreams to life. Let this ritual be a celebration of your creativity and a catalyst for achieving your goals.

LEO WANING GIBBOUS MOON

Inspire Others

LEO
WANING GIBBOUS MOON
QUICKIE
For the busiest of magical bees.

Busy Witch Ritual:

Look back at photos of yourself throughout the past and share the energy you're experiencing now with your past self.

Self-Care Tip:

Journal by candlelight to share your inspired efforts with the universe. Or, go for a walk at night and share in community with friends and family.

Affirmation:

As the Leo Moon wanes, I gracefully release what no longer serves my highest good. I trust in the process of transformation, knowing that each step back is a path forward to greater wisdom and strength. I am confident in my ability to feel the way I want to feel in my daily life.

Leo Waning Gibbous Moon Ritual: Artistic Expression

♌

This ritual for the Disseminating Moon in Leo is designed for solo practice but keeps the spirit of sharing and expression alive. Channel your creativity, express yourself through art, and then share your creation with others, embodying the proud and expressive energy of Leo.

You Need:

- Choose a variety of paints and brushes for your artistic endeavor.
- Prepare a canvas where you'll express your creativity.
- Collect crystals like Peridot, Sunstone, and Tiger's Eye to inspire creativity and confidence.
- Optionally, have your favorite beverage to enjoy while you create.

To Begin:

- Set up a comfortable area for painting. This could be a quiet corner in your home or a spot outdoors if the weather permits.
- Arrange your crystals around your canvas to enhance the creative energy.

The Ritual:

- Sit for a moment with your canvas and art supplies. Reflect on what you've learned and experienced during the past full moon phase.
- Set an intention for your art session. It could be to express a particular emotion, capture a memory, or simply to let your intuition flow.

- Set a timer for a designated period, like 5 or 10 minutes, to create a sense of playful urgency, much like the group activity.
- Start painting when the timer begins, allowing yourself to freely express whatever comes to mind. Don't overthink; just enjoy the process of creation.
- As you paint, imagine yourself roaring like a Leo lion, proud and unapologetic in your expression.
- Let the act of painting be both a release and a celebration of your unique insights and experiences.
- Once your painting session is complete, consider sharing your artwork with friends or family, either in person or digitally.
- Explain the inspiration behind your piece and what the process of creating it meant to you.
- Clean up your painting area, thanking the Leo energy and the Disseminating Moon for their inspiration.
- If you chose to enjoy a beverage, raise a toast to your creativity and the joy of sharing.
- Display your artwork in a place where you can see it regularly as a reminder of your creative spirit and the power of self-expression.
- Continue to find ways to share your experiences, insights, and creativity with others, whether through art, conversation, or other forms of expression.

This Leo Moon ritual adapts the communal joy of artistic creation into a personal practice of self-expression and sharing. By embracing the bold, creative spirit of Leo on your own, you honor your individuality and the importance of sharing your unique voice with the world.

LEO THIRD QUARTER MOON
Release and Redefine

LEO THIRD QUARTER MOON

QUICKIE
For the busiest of magical bees.

Busy Witch Ritual:

Let go of what hasn't served your creative journey. Write what you'd like to release on a piece of paper and color over it before tossing it away.

Self-Care Tip:

Redecorate a space or update your wardrobe to reflect your inner transformation.

Affirmation:

Under this Leo Third Quarter Moon, I embrace the courage to let go of the past and welcome change. I am empowered to reshape my life with confidence, creativity, and a heart full of joy. I actively envision feeling the way I want to feel and have the courage and resolve to allow it into my life.

Leo Third Quarter Moon Ritual: Love-Infused Chocolates

Ω

Leo's fiery and passionate influence is perfect for a bit of love magic. By creating your own love-infused chocolates, you're giving back to yourself and potentially adding a spark to your romantic life.

You Need:
- A candle in red, pink, or white to symbolize love and passion.
- Plain chocolates suitable for melting.
- Cinnamon for its properties of love and attraction.
- A silicone mold for shaping your chocolates.
- A double boiler or a heat-safe bowl and pot for melting chocolate.

To Begin:
- Choose a time when you can perform the ritual in your kitchen.
- Cleanse the area if you wish, perhaps with incense or by simply tidying up and setting a clear, positive intention.

The Ritual:
- Carve a symbol or word related to love into your candle or anoint it with oil.
- Light the candle on or near your stovetop, setting the intention for love and passion to infuse into your ritual.

- Set up your double boiler or heat-safe bowl over a pot of simmering water. Add the chocolates and gently melt them over low heat.
- As the chocolate melts, focus on the transformative energy of the fire element, symbolizing the awakening of love.
- Once the chocolate is melted, sprinkle in a bit of cinnamon.
- Stir the mixture clockwise three times. As you stir, state your affirmation about love. This could be focused on self-love, such as "I am worthy and deserving of love," or on romantic love, like "My relationship is filled with passion and understanding."
- Carefully pour the melted chocolate into your silicone molds.
- As you do this, visualize the love you desire filling each mold, ready to manifest in your life.
- Let the chocolates set until they are firm.
- When you eat them, do so with intention, savoring each bite and visualizing the love affirmation filling you up and overflowing into your life.
- Keep the candle and any remaining chocolates in a special place. Light the candle whenever you wish to remind yourself of the love affirmation.
- Share the chocolates with your partner if the ritual was focused on romantic love, or enjoy them yourself as a treat of self-love.

This is a delightful way to engage with the energies of love and passion. By creating love-infused chocolates, you're not only performing a magical act but also treating yourself to a sensory experience that reinforces your love energy. Let this ritual be a reminder of the joy and warmth that love, in all its forms, brings into your life.

LEO WANING CRESCENT MOON

Rest and Recharge

LEO
WANING CRESCENT MOON
QUICKIE
For the busiest of magical bees.

Busy Witch Ritual:

Take time to rest and recharge your batteries. Reflect on your journey and how it has fueled your creative fire. Drink cinnamon tea or add cinnamon to another drink and close this lunar cycle.

Self-Care Tip:

Spend a quiet evening enjoying a favorite movie or book to relax and recharge.

Affirmation:

Under the Waning Crescent Moon in Leo, I release my fears and embrace my inner strength. I am confident, radiant, and ready to welcome new beginnings with open arms and a fearless heart. I confidently envision my future and know that I have everything I need within me to feel the way I want to feel.

Leo Waning Crescent Moon Ritual: Sacred Dance

♌

Combine the restorative energy of the moon phase with Leo's vibrant, expressive nature and sacred dance. Rejuvenate and prepare for the new lunar cycle by embracing movement as a form of release and renewal.

You Need:
- Music and yourself!

To Begin:
- Set up a comfortable area where you have enough room to move freely. This could be in your living room, bedroom, or any space where you feel at ease to express yourself through dance.
- Play music that inspires and energizes you. Choose rhythms and melodies that speak to your soul and encourage fluid, expressive movement.

The Ritual:
- Stand in your dance space and take a few deep breaths. Set an intention for your dance, focusing on releasing the old and welcoming the new.

- Start your music and begin to move. Let your body flow naturally to the rhythm. Don't worry about getting the steps right; this dance is about expression, not perfection.
- As you dance, imagine yourself shedding any weight or burdens from the past lunar cycle. Visualize each movement making you lighter, freeing you from what no longer serves you.
- With each step and movement, picture yourself becoming more radiant, filled with new energy and potential for the upcoming lunar cycle.
- Embrace the fiery energy of Leo in your dance, allowing it to fuel your movements with strength and passion.
- When you're ready to end, stand still for a moment, feeling the energy you've created. Express gratitude to yourself for this time of rejuvenation and to the Leo energy for its vibrancy.
- Reflect on your experience with the dance. How did it make you feel? What emotions or insights came up?

This Waning Moon in Leo ritual is a celebration of renewal through movement. By engaging in sacred dance, you honor the restorative aspect of the Balsamic Moon and the expressive, joyful nature of Leo. Let this ritual be a reminder of the transformative power of your body and the beauty of embracing change with grace and vitality.

LEO RITUAL NOTES

LEO RITUAL NOTES

VIRGO

Virgo, the sixth sign of the zodiac, embodies meticulousness, practicality, and a deep sense of service. Embrace order and value precision, improvement, and usefulness. When the Moon is in Virgo it invites you to focus on the finer details, to organize your life for efficiency, and to engage in acts of service, all while maintaining a sense of wellness in your daily routines.

Virgo energy is both analytical and helpful. Yet, there are potential pitfalls. Sometimes the perfection-seeking nature of Virgo can lead to excessive criticism or a paralyzing fear of imperfection, making it difficult to appreciate the beauty of flaws or to accept when things are 'good enough.'

Just as Virgo energy can provide a framework for practical problem-solving and self-improvement, it can also lead to a sense of hyper-criticism, both of oneself and others. What begins as a quest for perfection and order can sometimes evolve into an overwhelming sense of never being satisfied. Strive for excellence and embrace imperfection.

Virgo Moon Toolkit

Here are some suggested tools for your Virgo moon ritual kit. Keep in mind that everything is optional and the only true requirement is your energy, magic, and belief!

- **Sun Sign Dates: August 23-September 22**

- **Candle Color: Brown**

- **Oil or Essence: Patchouli (for grounding and healing)**

- **Herb: Lavender (for peace and calm)**

- **Spell Focus: Organization and healing**

- **Element: Earth**   **Tarot: Pentacles**

- **Crystal: Moss Agate**

- **Mythology: Demeter and Persephone**

Virgo in My Chart

Refer to your birth chart and look for Virgo. It may be marked with this symbol: ♍

🌙 **House(s):**

🌙 **Planet(s):**

🌙 **Notes:**

Whenever the Moon is in Virgo, it will highlight this part of your birth chart and you may notice heightened emotions in this area or shadow aspects of your life or energy coming to the surface.

VIRGO NEW MOON

Set Intention with Purpose

VIRGO NEW MOON
QUICKIE
For the busiest of magical bees.

Busy Witch Ritual:

In a calm, organized setting, write down a practical and detailed list of things that will make you feel amazing. Focus on how these can bring more order and wellness into your life. Close your eyes and visualize yourself having everything on your list.

Self-Care Tip:

Enjoy a brief, focused meditation or a short walk to clear your mind and set your intention with precision.

Affirmation:

Under the New Moon in Virgo, I embrace clarity, precision, and purpose. I am grounded in my goals, organized in my actions, and ready to cultivate a life of harmony and well-being. I make decisions that easily allow me to feel the way I want to feel, knowing I am ready and capable.

Virgo New Moon Ritual: Beautiful Intention Setting

♍

Create a beautiful and harmonious space to nurture and ground your intention. Virgo's love for beauty, order, and perfection is the perfect inspiration for crafting an environment that not only pleases the senses, but also supports your goals and aspirations.

You Need:

- Select items that you find beautiful and uplifting. These could include plants, crystals, art pieces, candles, or even an exciting tablecloth or wall hanging.
- If your intention is mobile, consider creating a portable 'beauty kit.' This could be a small bag filled with items like miniature crystals, a small notebook, or a piece of inspiring artwork.
- Decide where you will focus your intention-setting efforts. This could be a specific area in your home or workplace, like your desk, kitchen, or a personal altar.

To Begin:

- Begin by clearing and decluttering your chosen space. Embrace Virgo's love for order and cleanliness, creating a fresh canvas for your ritual.
- As you clean, visualize yourself clearing away any mental or emotional clutter, making room for new beginnings.

The Ritual:

- Once your space feels ready, take a seat or stand comfortably within it. Take a few deep breaths to center yourself.
- Reflect on your intention for this lunar cycle. What do you wish to cultivate or achieve? How do you want to feel? How does this beautiful space support this intention?
- Visualize your intention taking root in this beautiful space. Imagine it growing and flourishing, supported by the order and beauty around you.
- Affirm your intention out loud or silently. You might say, "In this space of beauty and order, I plant the seeds of my intention, trusting in their growth and fruition."
- Spend a few more moments enjoying the beauty of your space, feeling gratitude for the peace and inspiration it provides.
- Conclude your ritual with a simple statement of gratitude or a closing gesture, like blowing out a candle or gently touching each item in your space.

By mindfully crafting a space that resonates with Virgo's aesthetic and practical nature, you set the stage for a lunar cycle filled with growth, clarity, and accomplishment. When your environment is treated as sacred you are more likely to feel the way you want to feel.

VIRGO WAXING CRESCENT MOON

Plan and Prepare

VIRGO
WAXING CRESCENT MOON
QUICKIE
For the busiest of magical bees.

Busy Witch Ritual:

Break down your goal into small, manageable tasks. Incorporate these tasks into your daily routine, connecting to the energy of your future along the way.

Self-Care Tip:

Prepare a healthy meal or organize a small area of your home to align with your intention or goal.

Affirmation:

As the Waxing Crescent Moon glows in Virgo, I nurture my intention and goal with meticulous care. Each small step I take is guided by practical wisdom and a deep connection to my inner truth. With the focused energy of Virgo on my side I always have what I need to feel the way I want to feel.

Virgo Waxing Crescent Moon Ritual: Intentional Space

♍

Combine the practicality of cleaning with the mindfulness of intention setting. Instead of succumbing to the urge to over-plan, use this time to physically and energetically clear your space, aligning it with your intentions.

You Need:

- Cleaning tools and products. Consider using natural or homemade cleaners to add an extra layer of intention.
- Choose decor items that align with your intention. For abundance, think of incorporating elements in green, red, and gold. For manifesting a dream vacation, gather images or items related to your desired destination.

To Begin:

- Select areas in your home that you feel most connected to your intention. This could be your workspace, living area, or even the entrance to your home.

The Ritual:

- Before you start cleaning, take a moment to focus on your intention. What are you hoping to manifest or cultivate during this lunar cycle?
- Visualize your intention clearly, imagining it taking shape and form in your life.

- As you clean each area, focus on the act of removing physical clutter as well as any mental or emotional blocks.
- Envision the good energy flowing into the space with each sweep, wipe, or rearrangement.
- Pay special attention to your front door area. A clean and welcoming entrance invites positive energy into your home.
- Consider adding a new decor element here that aligns with your intention.
- Once the cleaning is done, start placing your chosen decor items around your home.
- As you arrange each item, imagine it amplifying your intention. For example, placing green, red, and gold elements thoughtfully around your space to attract abundance.
- After you've finished, stand in the center of your home and take a few deep breaths.
- Feel the cleanliness and order around you, and visualize your intention growing in this nurtured space.
- Conclude with a statement of gratitude or affirmation, such as "I welcome growth and positive change into my life."
- Maintain the cleanliness and order in your space, seeing it as a physical representation of your internal state.
- Regularly spend time in the areas you've decorated, using them to meditate on and reinforce your intention.
- As the lunar cycle progresses, observe how the changes in your environment reflect the changes within you and your life.

This ritual in Virgo is a perfect blend of practical action and mindful intention. By transforming your living space into a physical manifestation of your goals, you create an environment that supports and nurtures your aspirations, allowing them to flourish.

VIRGO FIRST QUARTER MOON
Take Methodical Action

VIRGO FIRST QUARTER MOON
QUICKIE
For the busiest of magical bees.

Busy Witch Ritual:

Re-dedicate your yearly planner to your future self (or do it for the first time this year) and schedule specific times each day to work towards your goal this cycle.

Self-Care Tip:

Participate in a short, efficient workout or a cleaning session to maintain order and focus.

Affirmation:

Under the First Quarter Moon in Virgo, I embrace clarity and precision in my actions. I trust in my ability to make thoughtful decisions that align perfectly with my goal and how I want to feel. I am supported in my aspirations and have what it takes to move forward on my journey.

Virgo First Quarter Moon Ritual: Organizing Action

♍

This ritual for the First Quarter Moon in Virgo is designed to help you organize and prioritize the steps towards your intention or goal. It combines the grounding energy of Virgo with the First Quarter power of the moon to bring clarity and focus to your actions.

You Need:
- Three black or white spell or taper candles.
- Pen and paper for jotting down your thoughts and plans.

To Begin:
- If possible, find a quiet outdoor space where you can see the moon. This could be a garden, a balcony, or any safe outdoor area. Or sit inside and do this at any time of day, whatever works!

The Ritual:
- Begin by lighting the first candle. Stand with your arms raised towards the sky, either looking up at the moon or closing your eyes.
- Breathe deeply and feel the stretch in your body, connecting with the energy of the moon and the night.
- Spend a few moments in this position, breathing and stretching. Feel the warmth and energy flowing through your body, grounding you in the present moment.

- Light the second candle and then sit down comfortably.
- Close your eyes, take a deep breath, and focus on your intention. Reflect on the steps you've already taken towards it and what still needs to be done.
- Open your eyes and write down all the actions related to your intention, both completed and pending.
- Cross off the completed items. Then, number the remaining tasks in order of importance or urgency.
- Light the third candle. Take some time to schedule the remaining tasks. Consider when and how you will accomplish each one.
- Visualize yourself completing these tasks and your intention coming to fruition.
- Once you've planned your actions, spend a few moments in quiet reflection, letting the candles burn.
- You can choose to let the candles burn down completely or blow them out and relight them each day until the Full Moon as a reminder of your commitment.
- Keep your list of actions somewhere visible as a daily reminder of your intention and the steps you need to take.
- Regularly review and adjust your plan as needed, staying flexible and responsive to changes.
- As you complete each task, acknowledge your progress and celebrate your dedication to your intention.

This ritual is a grounding force, helping you to navigate the path towards your intention with confidence. As you move through the lunar cycle, remember that the journey towards your intention is as important as the destination, and each small step is a significant part of your overall success.

VIRGO WAXING GIBBOUS MOON

Analyze and Adjust

VIRGO
WAXING GIBBOUS MOON
QUICKIE
For the busiest of magical bees.

Busy Witch Ritual:

Journal on your progress this lunar cycle and then release the rest to the universe. Trust that you've done enough.

Self-Care Tip:

Enjoy a relaxing activity that allows you to think, like knitting or crafting, to keep your mind engaged and hands busy.

Affirmation:

As the Waxing Gibbous Moon illuminates the sky in Virgo, I trust in the process of refinement. I am patient and meticulous, ensuring every step I take brings me closer to my highest potential. I know I have what it takes to feel the way I want to feel this lunar cycle.

Virgo Waxing Gibbous Moon Ritual: Trust Affirmations

♍

Cultivate trust in the universe and release the need for control, a challenge often felt under Virgo's influence. By creating and embracing affirmations of abundance and trust, you align with the universe's flow, allowing your intention and goal to manifest naturally.

You Need:

- Pen and paper or a journal for writing your affirmations.
- A quiet and comfortable space where you can reflect without interruptions.
- You might want to light a candle or incense to create a peaceful environment.
- Consider playing soft, soothing music to help you relax and focus.

To Begin:

- Begin by reflecting on the areas of your life where you struggle to let go of control and trust in the universe's timing.
- Think about how Virgo's desire for organization and predictability might be influencing your ability to release and trust.

The Ritual:

- Start writing affirmations that resonate with your willingness to trust in the universe's plan. Use positive, present-tense language.

- You can use the suggested affirmation or create your own. For example, "I release control and trust in the flow of abundance," or "I am open to the universe's timing, knowing it brings me what I need."
- Once you have written your affirmations, read them aloud several times. Feel each word and let the meaning sink in.
- Visualize yourself living these affirmations, fully trusting in the universe and embracing the abundance that comes your way.
- Spend a few minutes in meditation, focusing on your affirmations. With each breath, imagine yourself letting go of control and opening up to trust and abundance.
- If your mind wanders to doubts or worries, gently bring it back to your affirmations.
- Conclude your ritual by expressing gratitude to the universe for its guidance and abundance.
- Keep your affirmations in a place where you can see them, such as on your mirror, desk, or altar.
- Revisit your affirmations as needed, especially when you find yourself struggling with trust or control. Read them daily for three days.

This Waxing Gibbous Moon ritual in Virgo is a gentle reminder of the power of surrender and trust. By acknowledging Virgo's tendencies towards control and counteracting them with affirmations of trust and abundance, you open yourself to the natural flow of the universe, allowing your intention and goal to manifest in perfect timing.

VIRGO FULL MOON
Celebrate and Declutter

VIRGO FULL MOON
QUICKIE
For the busiest of magical bees.

Busy Witch Ritual:

Celebrate every little success you've had and release the temptation to strive for perfection. Stretch your body and release tension.

Self-Care Tip:

Journal or create a list of accomplishments to visually appreciate your progress.

Affirmation:

Under the Virgo Full Moon, I embrace my journey towards perfection with grace. I am grateful for the wisdom and clarity it brings, guiding me to fulfill my goals with precision and care. I release the shadow aspect of Virgo and make space for the perfect elements that align with how I want to feel.

Virgo Full Moon Ritual: Declyttering for Clarity

♍

Declutter and organize your physical and mental space. Reflect on what serves your intention and what needs to be released, embracing Virgo's affinity for order and efficiency to create a harmonious environment that supports your goals.

You Need:
- Assemble any cleaning tools and products you'll need. Consider using eco-friendly or homemade cleaners for an extra touch of mindfulness.

To Begin:
- Select one or more areas that you feel most drawn to organize and declutter. It could be as small as a drawer or as large as an entire room.
- Before beginning, set an intention for this decluttering process. It could be to create a more peaceful living space, to clear mental clutter, or to make room for new opportunities.

The Ritual:
- Begin with a manageable area, like a drawer or countertop. This helps prevent feeling overwhelmed and allows you to see immediate results.

- Sort through items, asking yourself if each one serves your current intention or brings you joy. If not, donate, recycle, or discard it.
- Once you've decluttered an area, organize what remains in a way that makes sense to you and enhances the functionality of the space.
- Infuse this process with the energy of the Full Moon, allowing its light to bring clarity and purpose to your efforts.
- Consider starting a new healthy habit that aligns with your decluttered space. For example, if you've organized your kitchen, you might commit to cooking more nutritious meals.
- After you've finished decluttering, take a moment to appreciate the work you've done. Feel the sense of accomplishment and the new energy in your space.
- Reflect on how this physical decluttering can mirror a mental and emotional release, making room for new growth and opportunities.
- Maintain the order and cleanliness in the areas you've decluttered, seeing them as a physical manifestation of your internal state.
- As you move forward, notice how the decluttered and organized spaces impact your mood, productivity, and progress towards your goals.

This Full Moon in Virgo ritual is a powerful way to harness the moon's energy for creating a clear and purposeful environment. By decluttering and organizing your physical space, you mirror the process of clearing mental and emotional clutter, paving the way for a renewed focus on your intentions and aspirations.

VIRGO WANING GIBBOUS MOON
Experience Gratitude

VIRGO
WANING GIBBOUS MOON

QUICKIE
For the busiest of magical bees.

Busy Witch Ritual:

Stand with your eyes to the sky and allow your whole body to soften. Loosen your grip on perfectionism, the future, and expectation.

Self-Care Tip:

Enjoy a blog or book that inspires you aesthetically and gives you wisdom that empowers you to dream about the future.

Affirmation:

As the Virgo Waning Gibbous Moon illuminates the sky, I embrace the power of discernment and practicality in my life. I release what no longer serves me, making room for clarity and purpose. I trust in the process of refinement, knowing that each step I take leads me closer to my truest self and feeling the way I want to feel.

Virgo Waning Gibbous Moon Ritual: Cultivating Gratitude

♍

This ritual for the Disseminating Moon in Virgo is about acknowledging and expressing gratitude for the experiences and lessons of the past lunar cycle. Nurture yourself, appreciate the growth of your intentions, and give back to the earth, others, and yourself in meaningful ways.

You Need:
- Seeds for planting or a small indoor plant.
- Items for an outdoor altar, like safe food for wildlife.
- A list of people you want to thank or acknowledge.

To Begin:
- Choose activities that bring you joy and relaxation, such as dancing, walking, or a fun hobby.
- Identify a volunteer opportunity or plan a simple act of kindness, like paying for someone's coffee.

The Ritual:
- Begin by reflecting on the past lunar cycle. Acknowledge your wins, losses, and the lessons learned.
- Express gratitude for the opportunities the universe has provided to grow and manifest your intentions.

- Plant seeds or tend to your indoor plant in gratitude to the earth. As you do this, think about the growth and nurturing you've experienced.
- If creating an outdoor altar, arrange the food items mindfully, inviting wildlife to share in your gratitude.
- Reach out to those who have supported you. This could be through a thank-you note, a small gift, or a heartfelt message.
- Perform your act of kindness or volunteer, turning each action into a ceremony of gratitude.
- Engage in your chosen self-care activities. Allow yourself to fully enjoy these moments, embracing the joy and freedom they bring.
- As you participate in these activities, remind yourself of their importance in nurturing your mind, body, and soul.
- Conclude your ritual by sitting quietly, reflecting on the acts of gratitude you've performed.
- Feel the interconnectedness of giving and receiving gratitude, and how each act contributes to a greater cycle of kindness and appreciation.
- Reflect on how this ritual of gratitude has impacted your outlook and feelings, and carry this sense of thankfulness into the upcoming lunar cycle.

By consciously engaging in acts of gratitude, you not only honor the growth and lessons of the past lunar cycle, but also contribute to a cycle of positivity and kindness that extends beyond yourself. Let this ritual be a reminder of the joy and fulfillment that comes from expressing gratitude and nurturing your connections with others, nature, and yourself.

VIRGO THIRD QUARTER MOON

Honor Abundance

☽ ☽ ☽

VIRGO THIRD QUARTER MOON
QUICKIE
For the busiest of magical bees.

Busy Witch Ritual:

Let go of what hasn't worked or is no longer necessary. Use a stick and write a word that symbolizes this release in the earth.

Self-Care Tip:

Declutter your workspace or digital files to create a more efficient environment.

Affirmation:

Under the Virgo Third Quarter Moon, I find balance in letting go. I release perfectionism and embrace progress, trusting that each imperfection is a step towards growth. I am grounded in my purpose, aligning my actions with wisdom and practicality. I can clearly see the next logical step on my journey to feel the way I want to feel.

Virgo Third Quarter Moon Ritual: Honoring Abundance

Recognize and give thanks for the abundance in your life. Reflect on how you've cultivated this abundance. Whether in finances, time, energy, or relationships, create a space that honors them.

You Need:

- A candle to represent the light of abundance.
- Anointing oil or a sigil of gratitude for the candle.
- A crystal that resonates with abundance, such as Citrine or Jade.
- Items symbolizing your specific areas of abundance (e.g., a small clock for time, a penny for financial abundance).
- Pen and paper for jotting down your thoughts on abundance.

To Begin:

- Find a spot in your home where you can set up your altar, preferably somewhere you pass by often.

The Ritual:

- Begin by sitting quietly and reflecting on the areas of your life where you feel abundant.
- Write down your thoughts. How did you cultivate this abundance? Acknowledge both your efforts and the serendipitous events that contributed.

- Set up your altar in your chosen space. Place your candle at the center.
- Anoint the candle with oil or draw a sigil of gratitude on it, if you wish.
- Arrange the crystal and symbolic items around the candle, creating a visually pleasing and meaningful display.
- Light the candle, watching its flame as a symbol of the warmth and brightness of abundance.
- As the candle burns, express gratitude for each aspect of abundance you've identified. Feel appreciation for your ability to attract and cultivate these blessings.
- For the duration of the Third Quarter Moon phase, make it a practice to pause at your altar each time you pass by and light the candle when possible.
- Each pause is an opportunity to offer a nod or a moment of gratitude for the abundance in your life.
- At the end of the Third Quarter Moon phase, or when you feel the time is right, extinguish the candle for the final time this cycle.
- Reflect on how acknowledging abundance has impacted your mindset and feelings.

By taking the time to acknowledge the abundance in your life and the efforts that brought it into being, you align with the nurturing and analytical energy of Virgo, fostering a deeper appreciation for the blessings around you.

VIRGO WANING CRESCENT MOON
Prepare Mindfully

VIRGO
WANING CRESCENT MOON
QUICKIE
For the busiest of magical bees.

Busy Witch Ritual:

Take time to rest and rejuvenate. Reflect on the lunar cycle and how it has brought more order and wellness into your life.

Self-Care Tip:

Enjoy a quiet evening with a self-care routine, like a skincare ritual or reading a book on health and wellness.

Affirmation:

As the Virgo Waning Crescent Moon fades, I embrace the power of refinement and detail. I release what no longer serves me, creating space for clarity and precision in my journey. I trust in the process of subtle transformation, preparing for renewal and new beginnings. I release perfectionism but allow a discerning eye for detail on my journey through life.

Virgo Waning Crescent Moon Ritual: Mindful Preparation

♍

Prepare for the upcoming lunar cycle in a calming and structured way. It's a time to engage in activities that are both relaxing and preparatory, setting the stage for a cycle of mindful intention and action.

You Need:

- Your collection of herbs and magical essences or oils.
- A notebook or your magical book for copying rituals and spells.
- Materials to create affirmation cards, such as cardstock, pens, and any decorative items.
- Your calendar or planner for scheduling New and Full Moon activities.
- Meal planning tools and resources.
- A list of physical activities aligned with the lunar phases.

To Begin:

- Choose a quiet and comfortable area where you can carry out your tasks without distractions.
- Set up your space in a way that promotes calmness and focus.

The Ritual:

- Begin by tidying and organizing your herbs and oils. As you do this, appreciate the qualities of each item and how they contribute to your magical practice.

- This task is practical and contemplative allowing you to connect with your tools.
- Take time to hand write any new rituals, spells, or ideas you've come across for the next lunar cycle.
- Add these to your magical book and mark relevant dates in your calendar. This act of writing by hand is a mindful way to internalize these practices.
- Write an affirmation for each phase of the lunar cycle and create a set of cards.
- Decorate each card in a way that resonates with the energy of the respective lunar phase.
- Outline your activities for the New Moon and Full Moon, considering rituals or practices that align with your intentions.
- Meal plan with a focus on kitchen magic, choosing foods that correspond to the energies of the upcoming lunar cycle.
- Plan your exercise routine according to the lunar phases, incorporating more active workouts during yang phases and gentler practices like yoga during yin phases.
- Once you've completed your tasks, take a moment to appreciate the order and clarity you've brought into your space and practice.

This Waning Crescent Moon ritual in Virgo is a perfect blend of relaxation and preparation. By mindfully organizing and planning for the lunar cycle ahead, you embrace Virgo's love for detail and structure, setting yourself up for a cycle of intentional and harmonious practice.

VIRGO RITUAL NOTES

VIRGO RITUAL NOTES

LIBRA

Libra, the seventh sign of the zodiac, epitomizes balance, harmony, and justice. This sign invites you to see equilibrium in all aspects of life, appreciate beauty and art, and foster fair and equitable relationships. When the Moon is in Libra it encourages you to find harmony in your surroundings, to balance your personal needs with those of others, and to cultivate beauty and peace in your interactions and environment.

Libra energy is both diplomatic and aesthetically inclined. However, sometimes the pursuit of balance can lead to indecision or a tendency to avoid conflict, even when confrontation might be necessary.

Just as Libra energy can inspire a harmonious and artistic approach to life, it can also lead to a sense of complacency or a lack of authenticity in the quest to please everyone. What starts as a noble endeavor to create balance and harmony can sometimes result in a loss of individuality or a failure to address important issues. Libra's energy teaches us the importance of balance between maintaining peace and embracing honest, sometimes difficult, realities.

Libra Moon Toolkit

Here are some suggested tools for your Libra moon ritual kit. Keep in mind that everything is optional and the only true requirement is your energy, magic, and belief!

🌙 **Sun Sign Dates:** September 23-October 22

🌙 **Candle Color:** Pink

🌙 **Oil or Essence:** Rose (for harmony and beauty)

🌙 **Herb:** Thyme (for balance and justice)

🌙 **Spell Focus:** Relationships and balance

🌙 **Element:** Air   🌙 **Tarot:** Swords

🌙 **Crystal:** Lapis Lazuli

🌙 **Mythology:** Themis

Libra in My Chart

Refer to your birth chart and look for Libra. It may be marked with this symbol: ♎

🌙 **House(s):**

🌙 **Planet(s):**

🌙 **Notes:**

Whenever the Moon is in Libra, it will highlight this part of your birth chart and you may notice heightened emotions in this area or shadow aspects of your life or energy coming to the surface.

LIBRA
NEW MOON
Set Intention with Harmony

LIBRA NEW MOON
QUICKIE
For the busiest of magical bees.

Busy Witch Ritual:

In a peaceful setting, write down a goal and intention that fosters balance and harmony in your life. Focus on relationships or artistic pursuits.

Self-Care Tip:

Participate in a short, balancing yoga session or creating a small piece of art to set your intention with beauty and grace.

Affirmation:

I embrace the harmonious energy of the Libra New Moon, inviting balance and beauty into my life. I am open to forming meaningful connections and cultivating fairness in all my relationships. I balance how I want to feel with the complexities of life and take action accordingly.

Libra New Moon Ritual: Harmonizing Space

♎

Create a harmonious and beautiful living space that resonates with your soul. Balance personal joy with the happiness of those around you, guided by the aesthetic and balanced energy of Libra.

You Need:
- Natural elements like fresh flowers, seashells, or feathers to bring a sense of grounding and connection to nature.
- Candles or incense to create a serene ambiance.
- A journal or paper and a pen.

To Begin:
- Begin by tidying and beautifying your living space. Arrange it in a way that makes your heart sing, reflecting the harmony and beauty Libra stands for.
- Take a moment to sit quietly and absorb its energy. Notice the beauty and harmony you've created around you.
- Breathe deeply, allowing the calm energy of your space to fill you, grounding and centering your spirit.

The Ritual:
- In this beautiful setting, let your intuition guide you. What goal and intention feels right for this lunar cycle? What will bring harmony and joy not just to you, but also to those you care about?

- Consider how the balance of Libra can be reflected in your intention. How can you create equilibrium between your needs and the happiness of others?
- When you feel ready, write down your goal and intention. Phrase it positively and in the present tense, as if it's already happening.
- As you write, visualize your intention taking root in the harmonious energy of your space.
- Read your intention aloud, feeling its resonance in your harmonized space. Imagine it being amplified by the beauty and balance around you.
- You might want to place your written intention on an altar or a special spot in your space where you can see it regularly.
- Conclude your ritual with a few deep, grounding breaths. Express gratitude to the Libra New Moon for its guidance in finding balance and beauty.
- Blow out any candles or incense, carrying the sense of harmony and intention with you.

This New Moon in Libra ritual is a gentle invitation to embrace beauty, balance, and harmony in both your external environment and your internal world. By aligning your goal and intention with the energy of Libra, you set the stage for a lunar cycle filled with grace, equilibrium, and joy.

LIBRA WAXING CRESCENT MOON

Cultivate Alignment

LIBRA
WAXING CRESCENT MOON
QUICKIE
For the busiest of magical bees.

Busy Witch Ritual:

Reflect on how your daily interactions can nurture your intention. Hold your favorite crystal or stone in your hands and reflect on a time you received an act of kindness. Open yourself to paying it forward today.

Self-Care Tip:

Write a thoughtful note or message to someone you care about to strengthen your connections.

Affirmation:

As the Waxing Crescent Moon glows in balanced Libra, I embrace harmony in my thoughts and actions. I am open to fair and just connections, aligning my goal and intention with grace and diplomacy. With every step, I create equilibrium in my life. I bring even more harmony to my life by taking action to feel the way I want to feel.

Libra Waxing Crescent Moon Ritual: Intentional Alignment

♎

Use reflective journaling and tarot or oracle cards to explore alignment with your intention. It's time to make small adjustments, ensuring that your actions and mindset are in harmony with your goals, guided by Libra's focus on balance and equity.

You Need:
- Have a journal or notebook and a pen ready for your reflections.
- Choose a tarot or oracle deck that resonates with you for additional insights.
- Set up a quiet and comfortable space for journaling. You might want to light a candle or play soft, calming music to create a serene environment.

To Begin:
- Begin by sitting quietly, taking deep breaths, and tuning into the energy of the Waxing Crescent Moon in Libra. Feel its gentle influence encouraging balance and alignment.

The Ritual:
- Open your journal and write down the first prompt: "Where do I feel out of alignment with my intention?"
- Draw a tarot or oracle card for this prompt. Reflect on the card's message and jot down your thoughts and feelings.

- Move to the next prompt: "What can I release to find better alignment?" Draw a card and journal your insights.
- Then, ask yourself: "What can I embrace to find better alignment?" Again, draw a card and explore its significance in your journal.
- For the final prompt, "What changes could be made to help breathe life into this intention?" draw a card and contemplate actionable steps you can take.
- After completing your journaling, take a moment to review your responses. Summarize key insights or actions that can help align you more closely with how you want to feel.
- Affirm your commitment to these adjustments, recognizing that small changes can have a significant impact.
- Close your journal and take a few deep breaths, feeling grounded and aligned.
- Express gratitude to the Libra Moon for its guidance and to yourself for the willingness to seek balance and harmony.
- Implement the changes you identified, observing how they influence your journey towards your goal.

This Waxing Crescent Moon ritual in Libra is a practice in aligning your actions and thoughts with your how you want to feel. By engaging in thoughtful journaling and divination, you embrace Libra's harmonizing energy, ensuring that your path forward is balanced, harmonious, and true to your inner self.

LIBRA FIRST QUARTER MOON

Take Balanced Actions

LIBRA FIRST QUARTER MOON
QUICKIE
For the busiest of magical bees.

Busy Witch Ritual:

Focus on actions that promote balance and fairness to yourself. Close your eyes and visualize yourself working hard and then resting. Feel the energy in doing both and then get to it.

Self-Care Tip:

Listen to a short, harmonizing meditation or to music that brings peace and balance.

Affirmation:

Under the Libra First Quarter Moon, I find strength in balance. I take decisive action with fairness and grace, aligning my efforts with the scales of justice. My path is clear, my heart is open, and my actions reflect my commitment to harmony and balance.

Libra First Quarter Moon Ritual: Attraction Charm

♎

Utilize the properties of passionflower to create a charm that aids in attracting what you need to achieve your intention. Focus on specific actions and harness the calming, yet attraction-enhancing qualities of passionflower, aligning with Libra's energy of balance and attraction.

You Need:

- A spell bag or a small vial that can be worn as a necklace or carried with you.
- Dried passionflower, known for its properties of attraction and calming the mind.
- Choose a quiet place where you can perform your ritual undisturbed. You might want to light a candle or incense to set a serene mood.

To Begin:

- Begin by taking a few deep breaths and tuning into the energy of the First Quarter Moon in Libra. Feel its influence encouraging clarity, balance, and attraction.

The Ritual:

- Hold your spell bag or vial in your hands. Slowly fill it with dried passionflower, focusing on your intention and what you need to attract to achieve it.

- As you add the passionflower, recite the affirmation: "Under the first quarter moon, passionflower helps me fine-tune, and will attract just the right thing soon."
- Once filled, close the spell bag or seal the vial. Hold it between your palms, envisioning it glowing with the energy to attract the necessary elements for your intention.
- Visualize your intention clearly, imagining the steps you need to take and the outcomes you desire.
- Keep the charm with you as a constant reminder of your focused intention. Whether you wear it as a necklace or carry it in your pocket, let it serve as a symbol of the specific actions you need to take and the attraction energy you wish to harness.
- Conclude your ritual by expressing gratitude to the Libra Moon and the passionflower for their guidance and support.
- Spend a few moments in quiet reflection, feeling the charm's energy aligning with your intention.
- Reflect on the progress you make towards your intention, observing how the charm influences your actions and mindset.
- At the Full Moon, follow through with the dispersal of the passionflower back to the earth as a gesture of gratitude, or choose to keep it with you if you feel its energy is still actively supporting your journey.

By creating a passionflower charm, you are actively engaging with the energies of balance, attraction, and clarity that Libra offers, setting a clear path towards achieving your goals. Let this charm remind you of the power of focused intention and the support of the universe in manifesting your desires.

LIBRA WAXING GIBBOUS MOON
Refine and Beautify

LIBRA
WAXING GIBBOUS MOON
QUICKIE
For the busiest of magical bees.

Busy Witch Ritual:

Review your intention and/or goal for this lunar cycle and imagine yourself receiving what you desire and being surrounded by a harmonious bubble of light and support.

Self-Care Tip:

A beauty ritual, like a facial or styling your hair, to feel balanced and beautiful.

Affirmation:

As the Waxing Gibbous Moon glows in Libra's harmonious energy, I affirm my life is a beautiful balance of giving and receiving. I trust in the graceful flow of the universe to align my actions with justice, peace, and loving relationships. I am surrounded by beauty and fairness, and every step I take is guided by the scales of balance.

Libra Waxing Gibbous Moon Ritual: Balancing Thought and Trust

Ω

Examine and balance your self-talk to foster greater self-trust. Use tarot as a tool for introspection, helping you identify and overcome self-doubt, and align with Libra's energy of balance and harmony.

You Need:
- Choose a tarot deck that you feel connected to for this reflective exercise.
- Have a journal or notebook and a pen ready for your insights and reflections.

To Begin:
- Find a quiet and comfortable area where you can conduct your tarot spread without interruptions. You might want to light a candle or some incense to set the tone.

The Ritual:
- Begin by taking a few deep breaths, grounding yourself, and tuning into the energy of the Waxing Gibbous Moon in Libra. Feel its influence encouraging balance and clarity in your thoughts.
- Shuffle your tarot deck while focusing on your self-talk and the trust you have in yourself.

- Draw a card for each of the following prompts and lay them out in front of you:
    - How is my self-talk sabotaging my ability to trust myself?
    - What energy can I embrace to release doubt?
    - What energy can I embrace to nurture trust?
    - What would it look like for me to trust myself completely?
- Spend time contemplating each card and how it relates to the prompt. What messages or insights are they offering?
- Journal your thoughts, feelings, and revelations for each card.
- As you write, allow yourself to explore deeply how your current self-talk patterns might be impacting your self-trust. Be honest and compassionate with yourself.
- After reflecting on each card, think about practical ways you can integrate these insights into your daily life. How can you adjust your self-talk to be more supportive and trusting?
- Consider creating daily affirmations or mantras based on the positive energies identified in your tarot spread to reinforce trust in yourself.
- Once you've completed your journaling and reflection, take a few more deep breaths, feeling the balance and harmony of the Libra Moon.
- Express gratitude to the tarot for its guidance and to yourself for the willingness to seek balance and trust.
- Gently close your ritual space, perhaps by blowing out the candle or putting away your cards.

By using tarot as a tool for introspection and journaling to explore your inner dialogue, you embrace Libra's harmonizing energy, setting a foundation for greater self-confidence and trust in your personal journey.

LIBRA
FULL MOON
Celebrate and Reflect

LIBRA FULL MOON
QUICKIE
For the busiest of magical bees.

Busy Witch Ritual:

Create a list of things you are tolerating that make you feel out of balance and throw it away to release connection to them.

Self-Care Tip:

Attend an art exhibit, see a play, or listen to some live music to celebrate your progress.

Affirmation:

Under the radiant Full Moon in Libra, I embrace the energy of balance and harmony in my life. I celebrate the equilibrium of my inner and outer worlds, recognizing the beauty in all my relationships. With gratitude, I acknowledge the fairness and love that surround me, and I commit to nurturing these bonds with kindness and understanding.

Libra Full Moon Ritual: Balancing Tea

♎︎

Create and enjoy a special tea blend that promotes balance and alignment. It's a time to harmonize your mind, body, and soul, drawing on the energy of Libra and the illuminating power of the Full Moon.

You Need:

- Select herbs associated with Libra and the Full Moon, such as bergamot, lemongrass, thyme, jasmine, and rose. Ensure they are safe for consumption.
- Have hot water ready for brewing your tea.
- Choose a special mug that enhances the ceremonial aspect of the ritual.
- Optional: Include a candle and crystals like Morganite, Aventurine, Rhodochrosite, Moonstone, Clear Quartz, or Rose Quartz to enhance the energy of balance and harmony.

To Begin:

- Set up a comfortable and uncluttered area for your tea ceremony. This could be indoors in a peaceful corner or outdoors under the moonlight.
- Begin by clearing your mind and grounding yourself. Take deep, slow breaths, focusing on the flow of energy through your body.

The Ritual:

- Inhale and exhale for equal amounts of time, bringing balance between your body, mind, and spirit.
- As you prepare to make your tea, set an intention for it to bring peace and balance where it's needed in your life.
- Visualize this intention infusing the herbs as you brew your tea.
- Infuse your chosen herbs in hot water. As the tea steeps, imagine its properties harmonizing your inner being.
- If you're outside, let the light of the Full Moon shine over your tea, enhancing its balancing qualities.
- Drink your tea mindfully, focusing on absorbing peace and balance with each sip.
- Create your own ceremony around this experience, whether it's sitting quietly under the moon, lighting candles, holding crystals, or incorporating other magical tools.
- After finishing your tea, take a few moments to reflect on the sensations of balance and tranquility within you.
- Express gratitude to the Libra Full Moon for its harmonizing energy.
- Consider making this tea blend again during significant times or when you feel the need to restore balance in your life.
- Return the tea remnants to the earth when you have completed the ritual.

This Full Moon in Libra ritual is a beautiful way to connect with the energies of balance, harmony, and illumination. By crafting and enjoying a special tea blend, you engage in a mindful practice that nurtures your inner equilibrium, aligning your energies with the tranquil and balanced essence of Libra.

LIBRA WANING GIBBOUS MOON

Love and Harmony

LIBRA
WANING GIBBOUS MOON
QUICKIE
For the busiest of magical bees.

Busy Witch Ritual:

Seek an area of life where you can be more forgiving and harmonious.
Send love there.

Self-Care Tip:

Volunteer for a cause you believe in or participate in a community event to
spread harmony.

Affirmation:

As the Libra moon wanes, I gracefully release any imbalances and
disharmony from my life. I trust in the natural flow of giving and receiving,
knowing that each release creates space for new blessings. I cherish the
lessons learned and move forward with a heart full of gratitude and a spirit
of fairness. I find harmony on my journey to feel the way I want to feel.

Libra Waning Gibbous Moon Ritual: Cultivating Self-Love

♎

This ritual for the Disseminating Moon in Libra is about embracing self-love and gratitude. Recognize and appreciate your strengths and the beauty you bring to the world, balancing Libra's tendency to prioritize others over oneself.

You Need:
- A glass bottle or jar with a lid or cork.
- A pink candle to symbolize love and self-appreciation.
- Rose Quartz for love and Moss Agate for heart chakra healing.
- Dried rose petals representing love and beauty.
- A pen and two sheets of paper.

To Begin:
- Choose a quiet and comfortable area where you can perform your ritual undisturbed. You might want to light some incense or play soft music to enhance the atmosphere.

The Ritual:
- Place your crystals in the jar and fill it with dried rose petals.
- As you do this, start to focus on aspects of yourself that you are grateful for. Think about your strengths, talents, and the unique qualities you possess.

- On one sheet of paper, write an affirmation of love and gratitude to yourself. This could be a statement that acknowledges and celebrates your worth and beauty.
- Fold the paper and place it inside the jar with the crystals and rose petals.
- Light the pink candle and carefully let the wax drip onto the jar's lid or cork, symbolically sealing your affirmation of self-love inside.
- As the wax seals the jar, visualize sealing in all the positive energy and love.
- Spend a few moments in quiet reflection, holding the sealed jar. Feel the warmth of self-love and gratitude emanating from it.
- Acknowledge the balance and harmony within you, appreciating your ability to love yourself as deeply as you love others.
- Place the jar in a special spot where you will see it often, such as your bedroom, a personal altar, or a workspace.
- As you conclude the ritual, express gratitude to the Disseminating Moon in Libra for its guidance in finding balance and self-love.
- Blow out the candle, carrying the sense of self-appreciation and warmth with you.
- Whenever you feel the need for a reminder of your worth and self-love, return to your jar. Open it if you wish, read your affirmation, or simply let the sight of it fill you with warmth and love.

This Disseminating Moon ritual in Libra is a nurturing practice that encourages you to honor and appreciate yourself. By creating a physical representation of self-love and gratitude, you are reminded of your intrinsic value and the importance of caring for yourself.

LIBRA THIRD QUARTER MOON
Release and Rebalance

LIBRA THIRD QUARTER MOON
QUICKIE
For the busiest of magical bees.

Busy Witch Ritual:

Create a to-do list and a not to-do list. Feel into the harmony of knowing what's yours to do and what's not yours to do.

Self-Care Tip:

Engage in an activity that helps you find inner balance, like a long walk in nature or a session of deep breathing exercises, to realign your energies.

Affirmation:

Under this Libra Third Quarter Moon, I embrace the power of balance and decision-making. I let go of indecision and embrace clarity, trusting my inner wisdom to guide me towards harmony in all aspects of my life. I am at peace with my choices, knowing each step brings me closer to equilibrium and personal growth. I carry the vision of how I want to feel with me at all times.

Libra Third Quarter Moon Ritual: Release and Recreate Energy

♎

Release unused energy in creative and meaningful ways. Find balance, harmony, and beauty in letting go, and transforming this energy into something joyful and valuable.

You Need:

- If you're crafty, prepare materials for a project that brings you joy and allows you to channel unused energy creatively.
- Arrange a comfortable space for a deep conversation with a loved one. This could be over a cup of coffee or tea.
- Choose a crystal or stone to place on the table as a record keeper of the conversation's energy.
- Have incense and bells ready for the energy releasing part of the ritual.

To Begin:

- Begin by engaging in your chosen craft. As you create, focus on channeling any built-up, unused energy into the project.
- Visualize this energy being transformed into something beautiful and joyful, embodying the harmonious essence of Libra.

The Ritual:

- Invite a loved one to join you for a thoughtful conversation or simply engage with your inner self.

- As you talk, let the conversation flow naturally, delving into topics that are thought-provoking and meaningful. Or, explore your inner world.
- Place your chosen crystal or stone on the table to absorb the energy of this exchange.
- As you drink your coffee or tea, imagine it as a potion infused with the energy of your conversation or inner thoughts. Savor each sip, absorbing the positive, balanced energy.
- Light the incense, allowing its smoke to fill the space. Ring the bells to disperse any lingering energy that no longer serves you.
- As the smoke rises, visualize releasing any unused energy, letting it be carried away and transformed for use elsewhere.
- Conclude your ritual by expressing gratitude for the ability to release and recreate energy in harmonious ways.
- Keep the crystal or stone as a reminder of the positive energy and connections in your life, or of your beautiful inner world.
- Place the crafted item or the energy-infused crystal in a special place as a reminder of the ritual.
- Reflect on the experience of transforming unused energy and consider making this a regular practice during each lunar cycle.

This Third Quarter Moon ritual in Libra is a beautiful way to honor the cyclical nature of energy. By releasing what you no longer need and transforming it into something positive, you align with Libra's harmonizing energy, creating beauty and balance both within and around you.

LIBRA WANING CRESCENT MOON

Prepare for Renewal

LIBRA
WANING CRESCENT MOON
QUICKIE
For the busiest of magical bees.

Busy Witch Ritual:

As the lunar cycle comes to a close, prepare for the new cycle by setting the stage for renewed balance and harmony. Clear the energy of your home to prepare.

Self-Care Tip:

Practice a relaxing self-care routine, such as a warm bath with a soothing aroma or a gentle yoga practice, to nurture your sense of peace and readiness for the new cycle.

Affirmation:

As the Libra Waning Crescent Moon fades, I release what no longer serves me, creating space for new beginnings. I trust in the natural flow of life, knowing that every ending is a chance for rebirth. With grace and gratitude, I embrace the quiet moments of introspection, preparing for the renewal ahead.

Libra Waning Crescent Moon Ritual: Embrace Self-Awareness

♎

Deepen self-awareness and reflection. Go inward and assess your habits, goals, and self-perceptions, aligning with Libra's energy of balance and self-harmony.

You Need:

- Have a journal or notebook and a pen ready for your reflections.
- You might want to light a candle or some incense to create a calm and supportive environment.
- Soft, calming music can also set the right mood for deep reflection.

To Begin:

- Choose a quiet, comfortable space.
- Begin by finding a comfortable seated position in your chosen reflective space. Take a few deep breaths to center yourself and connect with the energy of the Balsamic Moon in Libra.

The Ritual:

- Open your journal and consider the provided questions, or simply close your eyes and ask yourself what you need to learn about yourself at this moment.
- Write freely, allowing your thoughts and insights to flow onto the page. Explore each question, being honest and open with yourself.

- Contemplate activities or habits that may be consuming your time without adding value to your life. How can you set boundaries or limit these activities?
- Think about a goal you've repeatedly set but haven't achieved. Reflect on the reasons behind this pattern and what changes might lead to success.
- Identify any false beliefs or misconceptions you hold about yourself. How are these impacting your ability to manifest your intentions?
- Dive into what you truly want in your life. Break down your desires into smaller components to understand the steps needed to achieve them.
- Acknowledge areas where you might be resisting change. Consider actionable steps you can take to embrace change and move forward.
- After completing your journaling, take a few moments to sit quietly, absorbing the insights you've gained.
- Express gratitude to yourself for the willingness to engage in self-reflection and to the Libra Moon for its balancing energy.
- Implement any actionable steps you've identified, observing how they influence your journey towards your goals and intentions.

This Libra ritual is a nurturing process of self-discovery and introspection. By taking the time to deeply reflect on your habits, goals, and self-perceptions, you embrace the harmonizing energy of Libra, fostering a deeper understanding of yourself and paving the way for meaningful change and growth. Let this ritual be a reminder of the power of self-awareness in creating a balanced and fulfilling life.

LIBRA RITUAL NOTES

LIBRA RITUAL NOTES

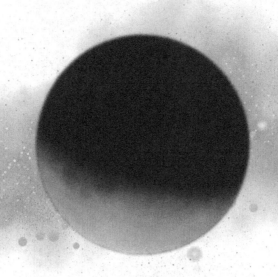

SCORPIO

Scorpio, the eighth sign of the zodiac, embodies depth, intensity, and transformation. Explore the mysteries of life, embrace change, and explore the depths of the human psyche. When the Moon is in Scorpio, it invites you to confront the truth, to embrace your inner strength, and to undergo profound personal transformations.

Scorpio energy is introspective and transformative. However, the intensity of Scorpio can lead to overwhelming emotions or a tendency to become secretive and withdrawn, even when openness might be more beneficial.

Just as Scorpio energy can drive a deep and transformative approach to life, it can also lead to a sense of brooding or an obsession with the unknown. What starts as a journey into the depths can sometimes become a labyrinth of complexity, making it hard to find the way back to simplicity and light. Scorpio's energy teaches us the importance of balance between diving deep and rising back to the surface. It reminds us that true transformation involves not just confronting our shadows, but also embracing the light that emerges from understanding them.

Scorpio Moon Toolkit

Here are some suggested tools for your Scorpio moon ritual kit. Keep in mind that everything is optional and the only true requirement is your energy, magic, and belief!

🌙 **Sun Sign Dates: October 23 - November 21**

🌙 **Candle Color: Dark Red**

🌙 **Oil or Essence: Myrrh (for mystery and depth)**

🌙 **Herb: Basil (for passion and protection)**

🌙 **Spell Focus: Transformation and intuition**

🌙 **Element: Water** 🌙 **Tarot: Cups**

🌙 **Crystal: Smokey Quartz**

🌙 **Mythology: Scorpius and Orion**

Scorpio in My Chart

Refer to your birth chart and look for Scorpio. It may be marked with this symbol: ♏

🌙 **House(s):**

🌙 **Planet(s):**

🌙 **Notes:**

Whenever the Moon is in Scorpio, it will highlight this part of your birth chart and you may notice heightened emotions in this area or shadow aspects of your life or energy coming to the surface.

SCORPIO NEW MOON

Transform

SCORPIO NEW MOON
QUICKIE
For the busiest of magical bees.

Busy Witch Ritual:

Light a deep purple or black candle, symbolizing Scorpio's mysterious energy. Visualize your future intensely, feeling yourself living in it.

Self-Care Tip:

Enjoy a relaxing bath with herbs or scents like patchouli or sandalwood to cleanse your aura and set your intention and goal with depth.

Affirmation:

Under the New Moon in Scorpio, I embrace transformation and rebirth. I am open to deep, meaningful change, trusting in the mysterious journey of my soul. With courage and resilience, I dive into my inner depths, unearthing hidden strengths and emerging renewed and empowered. I feel the way I want to feel and transform my life to support this.

Scorpio New Moon: Envisioning Transformation

♏

Focus on setting a powerful intention for transformation in a significant area of your life. It's about visualizing change from the current state to your desired future, using the transformative energy of Scorpio to facilitate this process.

You Need:
- Two pieces of paper.
- Pens, colored pencils, or markers for drawing and writing.
- Items to bind the papers together, such as candle wax or string.
- A tool for digging a small hole in the earth.

To Begin:
- Choose a quiet and private space where you can perform your ritual undisturbed. You might want to light a candle or incense to set a reflective mood.

The Ritual:
- On the first piece of paper, draw a figure representing the area of your life you wish to transform (e.g., a person, a wallet, a heart).
- Color, draw, or write on this paper to reflect the current situation in this area. Be honest and detailed in your depiction.
- On the second piece of paper, use the same figure to represent the transformed state you aspire to achieve.

285

- Again, use colors, drawings, or words to vividly illustrate what this transformation looks like. Focus on the positive changes and feelings associated with this new state.
- Fold the two papers together, symbolically merging the current state with the desired transformation.
- Use candle wax, string, or another method to bind them together, reinforcing your commitment to this change.
- Go outside and find a spot where you can safely and respectfully dig a small hole in the earth.
- Bury your bound papers in the hole, gently covering them with soil. As you do this, imagine the earth absorbing your intention and beginning the transformative process.
- Stand or sit quietly by the burial site. Close your eyes and visualize the transformation taking place. Imagine the energy of the earth nurturing and catalyzing the change from your current state to your desired one.
- Feel the powerful Scorpio energy aiding in this deep transformation, bringing intensity and depth to your intention.
- Once you feel your intention has been fully set and absorbed by the earth, express your gratitude to the New Moon in Scorpio for its transformative energy.

By visually representing your current state and desired transformation, and entrusting these to the nurturing power of the earth, you align with Scorpio's deep, transformative energy. Let this ritual be a reminder of your ability to evolve and change, embracing the transformative journey that life offers.

SCORPIO WAXING CRESCENT MOON

Nurture Your Inner Transformation

SCORPIO WAXING CRESCENT MOON
QUICKIE
For the busiest of magical bees.

Busy Witch Ritual:

Spend some time thinking about feeling the way you want to feel before you go to bed. Let your mind connect to the vision while you sleep.

Self-Care Tip:

Create a grounding meditation, visualizing roots growing from your feet, anchoring you as you embrace change.

Affirmation:

As the Scorpio Waxing Crescent Moon illuminates the night, I affirm my growing courage and intuitive power. I trust in the unfolding of my path, embracing each step with a fearless heart and a clear, insightful mind. I am ready to transform challenges into opportunities for growth and wisdom. I evolve into who I need to be to feel the way I want to feel.

Scorpio Waxing Crescent Moon Ritual: Release Limiting Beliefs

♏

Identify and release limiting beliefs that may hinder the realization of your goal and intention. Confront and discard negative self-talk, empowering yourself to move forward with confidence.

You Need:
- Paper and a pen for writing down limiting beliefs.
- A safe way to burn the paper, like a fireproof bowl or outdoor fire pit.
- Alternatively, a mirror for affirming positive beliefs.

To Begin:
- Choose a quiet and private area where you can reflect without distractions. You might want to light a candle or some incense to symbolize the transformative fire of Scorpio.

The Ritual:
- Write down your current limiting beliefs on paper, acknowledging their presence and your readiness to let them go.
- If you choose to burn the beliefs, do so safely. As the paper burns, visualize these self-imposed barriers disintegrating and losing their power over you.

- If you prefer to use affirmations, stand in front of a mirror. For each limiting belief, state its positive opposite out loud. For example, transform "I'm not good enough" into "I am capable and worthy."
- Whether you're watching the beliefs burn or speaking affirmations in the mirror, feel the power of Scorpio energizing your inner strength. Let this energy reinforce your belief in your ability to overcome and transform.
- Conclude by affirming your commitment to your goal and intention and your newfound strength. You might say, "I release what holds me back and embrace my power to succeed."
- Extinguish the candle or incense, carrying this sense of empowerment with you.

This Waxing Crescent Moon ritual in Scorpio is a wonderful way to confront and release the inner barriers that limit your potential. By actively discarding these limiting beliefs, either through the symbolic act of burning or through positive affirmations, you align with Scorpio's transformative energy, paving the way for success and self-empowerment.

SCORPIO FIRST QUARTER MOON

Gain Clarity

SCORPIO FIRST QUARTER MOON
QUICKIE
For the busiest of magical bees.

Busy Witch Ritual:

Picture yourself feeling the way you want to feel. What are you afraid of? Take action anyway.

Self-Care Tip:

Dress in a way you wouldn't normally and embody a fresh, exciting energy.

Affirmation:

Under the First Quarter Moon in Scorpio, I embrace my inner strength and resilience. I am determined to pursue my goals with passion and perseverance. My intuition guides me, and I trust in my ability to navigate through complexities with insight and courage. I transform into exactly who I need to be to feel the way I want to feel.

Scorpio First Quarter Moon Ritual: Water Scrying

♏

Utilize the ancient art of scrying with water to gain insight and clarity on the actions needed to manifest your intentions. Scorpio's deep, intuitive energy enhances the practice, guiding you towards understanding and decisive action.

You Need:
- A dark, plain bowl to be filled with water.
- Arrange any additional meditative or divination tools you prefer, such as candles, incense, or crystals, to aid in creating a contemplative atmosphere.

To Begin:
- Ensure you have a dimly lit environment to enhance the scrying experience.

The Ritual:
- Fill the dark bowl with water. The surface of the water will serve as your medium for scrying.
- If you're using candles, place them in a safe position where they can provide soft illumination without casting direct reflections on the water.
- Sit comfortably in front of the bowl. Take a few deep breaths to relax and center yourself.

- Allow your mind to calm and your thoughts to quiet. Focus on your intention and the guidance you seek.
- Gently gaze into the water. Let your eyes soften, not looking for anything specific, but remaining open to any symbols, patterns, or thoughts that arise.
- Be patient and open-minded. Scrying is a subtle art and may not yield immediate results. Trust in the process and in Scorpio's intuitive energy.
- After your scrying session, take some time to reflect on any images, symbols, or thoughts that came to you. Don't worry if nothing comes up immediately. Let the energy sink in and pay attention for signs, thoughts, or dreams later on.
- Consider how these insights relate to your intention and the actions you need to take during this moon phase.
- When you feel ready, gently bring yourself back to your surroundings.
- Express gratitude for any insights received and for the guidance of the Scorpio moon.
- Extinguish any candles or incense, and carefully dispose of the water, returning it to the earth if possible.
- Continue to meditate on the guidance received, allowing it to inform your steps as you work towards manifesting your intentions.

This First Quarter Moon ritual in Scorpio is a profound way to connect with your subconscious and the deeper intuitive currents within you. By engaging in the practice of water scrying, you open yourself to the mysterious and insightful energies of Scorpio, gaining clarity and direction for your journey ahead.

SCORPIO WAXING GIBBOUS MOON

Deepen Your Understanding

SCORPIO
WAXING GIBBOUS MOON
QUICKIE
For the busiest of magical bees.

Busy Witch Ritual:

Make herbal tea or infuse water with fruit. As you stir your potion, imagine trust filling the glass. Drink it and let self-trust move through your body.

Self-Care Tip:

Enjoy a session of deep, reflective yoga or a solitary walk at night to connect with your inner wisdom.

Affirmation:

As the Waxing Gibbous Moon illuminates Scorpio's depths, I trust in the transformative power of my journey. I am open to profound growth and embrace the changes that lead me closer to my truest self. My path is clear, guided by wisdom and the courage to evolve. I trust in the universe. I trust in myself.

Scorpio Waxing Gibbous Moon Ritual: Doubt into Trust

♏

Identify and transform self-doubt into trust in the universe. Use introspection and divination to rewrite the narratives that hold you back, aligning with Scorpio's themes of transformation and rebirth.

You Need:
- Have a journal or notebook and a pen ready for your reflections.
- Choose a tarot or oracle deck that resonates with you for additional insights.

To Begin:
- Find a quiet and comfortable space where you can reflect without interruptions. Consider lighting a candle or some incense to symbolize the transformative Scorpio energy.

The Ritual:
- Begin by taking a few deep breaths, grounding yourself, and tuning into the energy of the moon. Feel its influence encouraging deep transformation and the shedding of old patterns.
- Open your journal and consider these prompts: What stories of self-doubt are you telling yourself? How can these narratives be transformed to foster trust in the universe? What changes are needed to release doubt and embrace confidence?

- Draw a tarot or oracle card for each question. Reflect on the card's message and how it relates to your situation. Write down your thoughts and insights.
- Using the insights from your divination and reflection, start rewriting the stories you tell yourself. Transform negative, doubtful narratives into affirmations of trust and confidence.
- Visualize yourself letting go of old beliefs and embracing a new, empowered perspective.
- Read your rewritten narratives or affirmations aloud. Feel the power of your words as you actively choose to trust in the universe and your own transformation.
- Conclude your ritual by expressing gratitude for the guidance and insights received.
- Blow out the candle or incense, carrying the sense of transformation and renewed trust with you.
- Revisit your rewritten narratives and affirmations when faced with doubt or uncertainty.
- Observe how this shift in perspective influences your actions and mindset in the days following the ritual.

This Waxing Gibbous Moon ritual in Scorpio is a practice in confronting and reshaping the self-doubt that hinders your progress. By utilizing introspective journaling and divination, you harness Scorpio's transformative energy, paving the way for a renewed sense of trust and confidence in your path.

SCORPIO FULL MOON

Illuminate and Transform

SCORPIO FULL MOON

QUICKIE

For the busiest of magical bees.

Busy Witch Ritual:

Celebrate the revelations and transformations you've experienced. Carve a word for what you want to release into a small candle and burn it down.

Self-Care Tip:

Take a Full Moon bath using crystals like Obsidian or Moonstone around the tub, to honor your metamorphosis.

Affirmation:

Under the Scorpio Full Moon, I embrace my inner strength and resilience. I acknowledge the power of my emotions and use them as a force for positive transformation. I am deeply connected to my intuition, confidently navigating the depths of my soul's journey.

Scorpio Full Moon Ritual: Cultivating Self-Confidence

♏

This spell for the Full Moon in Scorpio is designed to enhance self-confidence and empower you to embrace your inner strength. Utilizing the transformative energy of Scorpio and the illumination of the Full Moon, this ritual helps you to affirm your personal power.

You Need:
- A shallow dish filled with water.
- A candle that can stand taller than the water level in the dish.
- Lemon balm, known for its properties of healing and confidence-boosting.
- Optional: Citrine chips and an uplifting flower essence for the confidence spray.

To Begin:
- Set up your ritual in a space where you feel comfortable and empowered.

The Ritual:
- Position the shallow dish of water in the center of your sacred space.
- Carefully place the candle in the center of the dish, ensuring it stands securely.

- As you light the candle, focus on the area of your life where you seek more confidence. Visualize yourself conquering challenges and radiating self-assurance.
- Sprinkle lemon balm around the candle in the water while affirming, "I am light, my confidence is bright, and so it is on this Full Moon night."
- Allow the candle to burn down completely during the ritual or over the remaining moon cycle. As it burns, imagine its light symbolizing the growth of your confidence and power.
- Once the candle has completely burned down, carefully filter out the lemon balm from the water.
- Transfer the infused water to a spray bottle. Optionally, add Citrine chips and a few drops of an uplifting flower essence to enhance its properties.
- Use this spray whenever you need a boost of confidence, spraying it around your aura or in your space.
- Conclude your ritual by expressing gratitude to the Scorpio Full Moon for its empowering energy.
- Feel the strength and confident energy within you, ready to face challenges with newfound assurance.
- Keep the confidence spray in a place where you can easily access it for regular use.

This Full Moon in Scorpio spell is a powerful way to harness the moon's energy for enhancing self-confidence and personal power. By creating a ritual space that combines the elements of water, candlelight, and lemon balm, you align with Scorpio's deep, transformative energy, setting the stage for personal growth and empowerment.

SCORPIO WANING GIBBOUS MOON
Old Becomes New

SCORPIO
WANING GIBBOUS MOON
QUICKIE
For the busiest of magical bees.

Busy Witch Ritual:

Share your progress with the universe by speaking about your transformation this cycle out loud or in your mind. Then anoint your chakras with a dab of salt water to release attachment to the first half of the cycle.

Self-Care Tip:

Engage in a creative activity that allows you to express your inner transformations, like painting or writing.

Affirmation:

In the Waning Gibbous Moon of Scorpio, I release what no longer serves me. I let go of old fears and embrace the wisdom gained from my experiences. I trust in the process of renewal, welcoming healing and transformation into my life.

Scorpio Waning Gibbous Moon Ritual: Old Into New

♏

Focus on the theme of transformation and rebirth. Take items in your home that have outlived their original purpose and creatively repurpose them, aligning with Scorpio's energy of renewal and the Waning Moon's preparation for a new cycle.

You Need:
- Look around your home for items that are no longer in use, such as worn-out clothes, chipped mugs, or old throws.
- Choose items that hold sentimental value or have the potential for repurposing.

To Begin:
- Set up a space where you can work on transforming these items. Ensure it's comfortable and has enough room for your project.

The Ritual:
- Begin by taking a few deep breaths, grounding yourself, and tuning into the transformative energy of Scorpio and the reflective energy of the Waning Moon.
- Choose the item you feel most drawn to repurpose. Hold it in your hands and reflect on its past use and the memories associated with it.
- Imagine the new form this item could take. What could it become that would bring joy or utility to your life? Visualize the transformation.

- Start repurposing the item, whether it's sewing a new cushion cover, turning a mug into a planter, or any other creative idea you have. As you work, focus on the theme of rebirth and renewal.
- As you transform the item, affirm aloud: "As I give new life to this object, I embrace the cycles of change and renewal in my own life. With each change, I grow and transform."
- Once your project is complete, take a moment to appreciate your work. Thank the Scorpio moon for its transformative energy.
- Place the repurposed item in a special place in your home as a symbol of your creativity and the power of transformation.
- Use or display the transformed item as a reminder of the ritual and the power of renewal.
- Reflect on other areas of your life that might benefit from a similar transformation or renewal.
- Carry the spirit of creativity and transformation into the upcoming lunar cycle, allowing it to inspire new intentions and fresh starts.

This Waning Moon ritual in Scorpio is a beautiful way to physically manifest the themes of transformation and rebirth in your daily life. By repurposing an item, you not only honor its past but also give it a new purpose, mirroring the process of personal growth and renewal. Let this ritual be a reminder of the endless possibilities for transformation that lie within and around you, and the power of creativity to turn the old into something new and beautiful.

SCORPIO THIRD QUARTER MOON

Let Go of the Old Self

SCORPIO THIRD QUARTER MOON
QUICKIE
For the busiest of magical bees.

Busy Witch Ritual:

Identify aspects of your old self that no longer serve you. Consciously release these, allowing for your renewed self to emerge. Clean an area of your home that is not in alignment with future you and discard anything that needs to be let go of.

Self-Care Tip:

Enjoy a cleansing ritual, perhaps with sound or a purifying bath, to symbolize shedding the old layers.

Affirmation:

As the Scorpio Third Quarter Moon illuminates the sky, I embrace the power of transformation. I release old patterns and welcome change, knowing each ending is a new beginning. I am resilient, adaptable, and ready for growth. I shed old ways of being to make space for new ones that allow me to feel the way I want to feel.

Scorpio Third Quarter Moon Ritual: The Phoenix Release

♏

Embrace the transformative energy of the Phoenix. It's a time for reflection, decision making, and releasing what no longer serves you through the empowering act of dance.

You Need:
- A candle and incense to set a transformative atmosphere.
- Music that resonates with your spirit and awakens your inner Phoenix.

To Begin:
- Choose a space where you feel free and uninhibited, whether indoors or outdoors. Ensure it's safe for movement and expressive dancing.
- Begin by lighting the candle and incense, inviting the deep, intuitive energy of Scorpio into your space. Feel the presence of the transformative Phoenix within you.

The Ritual:
- Play the music that makes you feel connected to your core – something that stirs feelings of empowerment, sensuality, and attunement with your true self. If you're playing an instrument, let your intuition guide your melody.

- Start dancing in whatever way feels natural to you. Let your body move freely, expressing all the emotions, thoughts, and energies you wish to release. Dance to let go, to give thanks, and to say goodbye to what no longer serves you.
- Allow the dance to be your meditation, a physical manifestation of your internal purging process.
- As your dance naturally slows, move into a state of surrender. Gently bring yourself to a seated or lying position in your sacred space.
- Breathe deeply and steadily, transitioning from the physical release to a state of stillness and receptivity.
- In this quiet, meditative state, express your gratitude for the experience and for the energies that have supported you in this process of release.
- Reflect on the space you've created within yourself for new beginnings and possibilities.
- Contemplate what you wish to invite into this renewed space.
- Conclude your ritual by affirming your readiness for renewal and transformation. You might say, "I embrace the rebirth that follows release. I am ready for the new that awaits."
- Extinguish the candle and incense, carrying the sense of renewal and potential with you.

Connect with the transformative energy of the Phoenix. By engaging in a ritual dance of release, you honor the process of letting go and create space for new energies to enter your life. Remember your resilience, strength, and the ever-present potential for rebirth and renewal within you.

SCORPIO WANING CRESCENT MOON

Reflect and Renew

SCORPIO
WANING CRESCENT MOON
QUICKIE
For the busiest of magical bees.

Busy Witch Ritual:

Feel into your emotional body and contemplate what you wish to seek or transform in the next cycle.

Self-Care Tip:

Enjoy a quiet evening of self-reflection, perhaps with a journal or a meditative practice, to internalize the lessons learned and prepare for renewal.

Affirmation:

Under the Waning Scorpio Moon, I let go of fears and embrace my inner strength. I trust in the natural flow of life, releasing what no longer serves me, and making space for new, empowering experiences. I transform into the person with the resilience and power to feel the way I want to feel.

Scorpio Waning Crescent Moon Ritual: Embrace Transformation

♏︎

Explore the depths of your inner self, embrace the darkness and the transformative power it holds. Reflect on your journey, acknowledge your achievements, and prepare for the rebirth that comes with the New Moon.

You Need:
- A mirror for self-reflection.
- A candle or battery-operated candle for dim illumination.
- Incense or a burning herb for smoke and cleansing.
- A journal for recording insights.
- Tarot or Oracle cards for intuitive guidance.
- Music with slow, rhythmic drumming to connect with the heartbeat of the earth.

To Begin:
- Set up your space in a dark room where the candlelight can softly illuminate your surroundings. Arrange your mirror, candle, and incense in a way that feels sacred and conducive to introspection.
- Begin by playing slow, deep music or rhythmic drumming to set the tone. Allow the rhythm to sync with your heartbeat, creating a connection between you and the earth's natural pulse.

The Ritual:

- Light your candle and incense, letting the gentle light and smoke fill the space. The dim light and the swirling smoke create an atmosphere conducive to introspection and transformation.
- Stand or sit in front of the mirror. Let the candlelight and smoke slightly distort your image, adding to the mystical experience.
- Gaze deeply into your own eyes. Reflect on your journey, the challenges you've overcome, and the growth you've experienced.
- Ask yourself, "Who am I at this moment? What parts of me are asking for transformation?" Listen to the responses that arise from deep within.
- Trust the feelings and intuitions that surface, even if they don't form coherent sentences. Let the experience be more about feeling than articulating.
- Draw cards from your Tarot or Oracle deck while continuing to gaze into the mirror. Let each card guide you to deeper understanding and clarity about your transformational needs.
- Trust your first impressions and intuitive responses to the cards.
- Write down your reflections, feelings, and insights from the mirror gazing and card reading in your journal. The process of recording helps solidify your inner discoveries.
- Conclude the ritual by expressing gratitude for the insights gained and for your own resilience and strength.
- Extinguish the candle and incense, feeling a sense of completion and readiness for the new cycle ahead.

Connect with your innermost self and embrace the transformative power of introspection and self-discovery. By engaging in this reflective practice, you honor the cycle of growth and renewal inherent in your journey, preparing yourself for the new beginnings that await.

SCORPIO RITUAL NOTES

SCORPIO RITUAL NOTES

SAGITTARIUS

Sagittarius, the ninth sign of the zodiac, embodies the spirit of adventure, a thirst for knowledge, and an unquenchable optimism. Explore the unknown, seek truth, and embrace a journey that expands your horizons both physically and mentally. Sagittarius energy encourages you to aim high, to pursue your aspirations with a sense of wanderlust, and to view life as a grand adventure filled with endless possibilities.

Sometimes the archer's quest for freedom and exploration can lead to a sense of restlessness or a disregard for boundaries, making it difficult to commit or to appreciate the beauty of the present moment. What starts as a pursuit of truth and experience can sometimes evolve into an avoidance of deeper emotional connections and responsibilities.

Sagittarius's energy teaches us the importance of exploring beyond our comfort zones while remaining connected to our roots and loved ones. It reminds us that true wisdom involves not just the accumulation of knowledge, but also understanding and empathy towards the diverse experiences of others.

Sagittarius Moon Toolkit

Here are some suggested tools for your Sagittarius moon ritual kit. Keep in mind that everything is optional and the only true requirement is your energy, magic, and belief!

🌙 **Sun Sign Dates: November 22 - December 21**

🌙 **Candle Color: Purple**

🌙 **Oil or Essence: Sage (for wisdom and adventure)**

🌙 **Herb: Mint (for expansion and luck)**

🌙 **Spell Focus: Exploration and philosophy**

🌙 **Element: Fire**   🌙 **Tarot: Wands**

🌙 **Crystal: Labradorite**

🌙 **Mythology: The Archer, The Centaur**

Sagittarius in My Chart

Refer to your birth chart and look for Sagittarius. It may be marked with this symbol: ♐

🌙 **House(s):**

🌙 **Planet(s):**

🌙 **Notes:**

Whenever the Moon is in Sagittarius, it will highlight this part of your birth chart and you may notice heightened emotions in this area or shadow aspects of your life or energy coming to the surface.

SAGITTARIUS NEW MOON
Set Your Sights High

SAGITTARIUS NEW MOON
QUICKIE
For the busiest of magical bees.

Busy Witch Ritual:

Light a purple or red candle, symbolizing Sagittarius's expansive energy. Write down a grand, adventurous goal and intention that sparks your excitement. Visualize it with optimism and trust in your journey.

Self-Care Tip:

Participate in a session of stretching or outdoor activity to invigorate your body and align your intention with Sagittarius's adventurous spirit.

Affirmation:

Under the New Moon in Sagittarius, I embrace the journey of growth and exploration. I set a goal and intention that ignites my adventurous spirit and open my heart to the endless possibilities that await. I look for opportunities to feel the way I want to feel and always pick myself up when I get knocked down. I radiate optimism easily.

Sagittarius New Moon Ritual: Visionary List

Embrace the sign's optimistic and adventurous spirit. Envision new possibilities and set a goal and intention that expand your horizons, aligning you with Sagittarius's expansive, exploratory energy.

You Need:
- A journal or paper for your lists.
- A candle in a color that resonates with Sagittarius' fiery energy (red, purple, silver, or white).
- A comfortable and quiet space where you can reflect and dream.

To Begin:
- Begin by lighting your chosen candle. As you watch the flame, invite the energetic and expansive spirit of Sagittarius into your space.

The Ritual:
- Take a few deep breaths to center yourself. Reflect on the concept of new beginnings and the adventurous energy of the New Moon in Sagittarius.
- Start with your first list: jot down everything you've always wanted to do but haven't yet. Let your imagination roam without limitations.
- Move on to your second list: places you've dreamed of visiting. Visualize each destination and the experiences you wish to have there.

- If you feel stuck or unsure, close your eyes while sitting near the candle. Let its warmth and light inspire you. Open yourself to the expansive energy of Sagittarius and Jupiter.
- As ideas come to you, add them to your lists. There are no wrong answers here; this is about exploring your deepest desires.
- Look over your lists and choose one item that excites you the most. Make a commitment to yourself to pursue this adventure or goal.
- Visualize yourself taking the steps to make this dream a reality, fueled by the New Moon's energy.
- Conclude by expressing gratitude for the inspiration and clarity received. Feel the optimism and excitement for the adventures ahead.
- Extinguish the candle, carrying the energy of your experience with you.
- Keep your lists in a place where you can see them regularly. They are a reminder of your adventurous spirit and the intentions set under the Sagittarius New Moon.
- Start planning or taking small steps towards the adventure or goal you chose. This could be researching, making a budget, or setting timelines.

This New Moon in Sagittarius ritual is a powerful way to harness the sign's love for exploration and growth. By creating visionary lists and choosing an adventure to embark upon, you align with the expansive and optimistic energy of Sagittarius, setting the stage for a journey of discovery and fulfillment in the lunar cycle ahead.

SAGITTARIUS WAXING CRESCENT MOON
Chart Your Path

SAGITTARIUS
WAXING CRESCENT MOON
QUICKIE
For the busiest of magical bees.

Busy Witch Ritual:

Outline practical steps towards your grand goal and intention. Visualize yourself completing them.

Self-Care Tip:

Enjoy a brief, mindful walk outdoors, connecting with nature to maintain the expansive energy of Sagittarius.

Affirmation:

As the Waxing Crescent Moon shines in Sagittarius, I trust in the path of discovery and adventure. I take bold steps towards my dreams, guided by optimism and the promise of new horizons. I can see myself feeling the way I want to feel and set out on the path to make it so.

Sagittarius Waxing Crescent Moon Ritual: Embrace Your Vision

Dare to dream big and confront the fears that come with such a grand vision. Align with Sagittarius's adventurous and optimistic spirit, visualizing your greatest dream and acknowledging the challenges that may arise.

You Need:

- A journal or paper and a pen for writing.
- A comfortable and quiet space where you can dream without limits.
- Items that inspire and represent your dream (photos, symbols, etc.).

To Begin:

- Set up your space in a way that feels open and conducive to expansive thinking. You might want to include items that symbolize growth, exploration, and adventure.
- Begin by relaxing in your space. Take deep breaths to clear your mind and open your heart to limitless possibilities.
- Think about your biggest dream, the one that feels almost too grand to achieve. Visualize it in vivid detail: the people, the environment, your emotions, and the sensations.

The Ritual:

- In your journal, start describing your dream as if it's already happening. Write about how your life looks, who you're with, how you feel, what you're doing, and where you are.

- Let your imagination flow freely, capturing every aspect of this dream on paper.
- Reflect on the aspects of your dream that scare you. Write them down. Acknowledge these fears as part of the journey towards your dream.
- Consider why these fears exist and how they are tests of your commitment to your dream.
- For each fear, write a statement of how you can overcome or address it. Turn these fears into stepping stones towards your dream.
- Affirm your strength and ability to handle these challenges, drawing on the bold energy of Sagittarius.
- Think about small steps you can start taking now to move closer to your dream. Write these down as actionable goals.
- Commit to taking at least one small step in the coming days.
- Conclude by reading aloud your dream and the steps you'll take to achieve it. Feel the power of your words and the support of the Waxing Crescent Moon in Sagittarius.
- Express gratitude for the clarity and courage gained from this ritual.
- Keep your written dream and action steps in a place where you can regularly see them as a reminder of your commitment.
- Start implementing the small steps you've identified, keeping the vision of your dream alive in your daily life.

By daring to dream big and confronting the fears associated with such dreams, you align with the expansive energy of Sagittarius, setting the stage for a journey of growth and fulfillment in the lunar cycle ahead. Embrace the journey with the confidence and enthusiasm characteristic of Sagittarius, and watch as your biggest dream starts to unfold into reality.

SAGITTARIUS FIRST QUARTER MOON
Embrace New Experiences

SAGITTARIUS FIRST QUARTER MOON

QUICKIE

For the busiest of magical bees.

Busy Witch Ritual:

Go outside and draw an arrow in the dirt while thinking of hitting your goal and feeling the way you want to feel.

Self-Care Tip:

Engage in a new physical activity or a fun, adventurous workout to keep your energy levels high and your spirit adventurous.

Affirmation:

Under the Sagittarius First Quarter Moon, I embrace the courage to face challenges head-on. My actions are fueled by my vision, leading me towards growth and expansion with confidence and enthusiasm. I take chances and know that it takes continuous action to feel the way I want to feel.

Sagittarius First Quarter Moon Ritual: The Action Spell

Harness the sign's fiery energy and motivation. Take decisive action towards your goals, using a multisensory spell to ignite your drive and determination.

You Need:

- Cinnamon incense, a cinnamon candle, or cinnamon essential oil for its stimulating properties.
- Pen and paper for writing your intentions and action steps.
- Matches or a lighter and a safe burn dish.
- A song that energizes and uplifts you.

To Begin:

- Set up your space in a way that feels energizing and empowering. You might want to include items that symbolize action and success.
- Begin by creating your sacred space in a way that feels right for you. This could involve clearing the area, setting up your items, or performing a brief grounding exercise.

The Ritual:

- Light your chosen cinnamon scent to fill the air with its invigorating aroma. Allow the scent to energize and motivate you.

- On the paper, write down what you wish to accomplish during this moon cycle. Be specific and bold in your actions and how you want to feel.
- Then, list all the immediate actions you can take to start manifesting this intention. Think of practical, achievable steps.
- Turn on your chosen song, one that really gets your energy flowing. As the music plays, dance freely and passionately, visualizing yourself taking action and achieving your goals.
- As you dance, feel the fiery energy of Sagittarius fueling your movements and intentions.
- Safely burn the paper with your written intentions and actions in the burn dish. As it burns, imagine releasing your intention, goal, or actions into the universe, transforming them into reality.
- When the song ends, raise your arms to the sky and affirm, "And so it is." Feel the certainty that your actions will lead to success.
- Extinguish the incense or candle safely.
- Take immediate action on at least one of the steps you listed. The energy of the ritual should propel you forward.

This First Quarter Moon ritual in Sagittarius is a dynamic way to kickstart your journey towards your goals. By combining the fiery energy of cinnamon with the power of music and dance, you create a potent spell for action and success. Embrace the adventurous spirit of Sagittarius and watch as your intention and goal begin to manifest in exciting and tangible ways.

SAGITTARIUS WAXING GIBBOUS MOON
Broaden Your Horizons

SAGITTARIUS
WAXING GIBBOUS MOON
QUICKIE
For the busiest of magical bee.s

Busy Witch Ritual:

Review your progress and look for ways to expand your approach. Close your eyes and invite in unexpected wisdom.

Self-Care Tip:

Practice a relaxation technique like muscle relaxation or guided imagery to balance Sagittarius's expansive energy with inner peace.

Affirmation:

I embrace the expansive journey of my soul, trusting that each step I take under the Sagittarius Waxing Gibbous Moon leads me to greater wisdom, freedom, and adventure. I trust that my desire and actions will get me exactly where I need to go.

Sagittarius Waxing Gibbous Moon Ritual: Embrace the Fire

Channel the fiery, expansive energy of Sagittarius into physical activity, balancing the yin energy of the lunar phase with the yang energy of the sign. Engage in physical exertion as a means of trusting and preparing for conscious creation.

You Need:
- Select an activity that resonates with Sagittarius's fiery nature and your personal preferences. This could be a hike, vigorous housework, a dance party, or any other form of physical exercise that gets your heart pumping and energy flowing.

To Begin:
- Set up your space or choose a location that allows for free movement and expression. If indoors, you might want to create room for movement and have water nearby to stay hydrated.
- Begin by grounding yourself and focusing on your intention for this lunar cycle. Acknowledge the Waxing Gibbous Moon's energy of trust and anticipation.

The Ritual:
- Light a candle or incense as a symbol of Sagittarius's fire.

- Start your chosen physical activity. Let yourself fully engage in the movement, feeling the fiery energy of Sagittarius fueling your actions.
- As you exercise, visualize the energy you're generating as a powerful force aiding the manifestation of your lunar intention.
- After your physical activity, take a moment to cool down and meditate. Breathe deeply, allowing the yin energy of the Waxing Gibbous Moon to permeate your being.
- Reflect on the balance of action (yang) and trust (yin), understanding that both are necessary for bringing your intentions to fruition.
- Affirm aloud or in your mind: "With the fire of Sagittarius, I energize my intentions. With the trust of the Waxing Gibbous Moon, I welcome their manifestation."
- Conclude your ritual by expressing gratitude for the strength and clarity gained. Feel the harmony between your physical exertion and the lunar energy.
- Extinguish the candle or incense, carrying the sense of balanced energy with you.

This Waxing Gibbous Moon ritual in Sagittarius is a powerful way to harness the sign's dynamic energy. By engaging in physical activity, you not only honor the fiery nature of Sagittarius, but also create a balance with the introspective energy of the lunar phase, paving the way for the successful realization of your intention and goal.

SAGITTARIUS FULL MOON

Self-Confidence and Freedom

SAGITTARIUS FULL MOON
QUICKIE
For the busiest of magical bees.

Busy Witch Ritual:

What would you love the freedom to do right now? Light a candle or make an outdoor fire. Imagine the flame creating the path.

Self-Care Tip:

Spend time under the moonlight, perhaps with a small fire or candles, to honor your achievements and the free spirit of Sagittarius. Enjoy your favorite music or read.

Affirmation:

Under the illuminating Sagittarius Full Moon, I celebrate my journey towards truth and freedom, feeling the universe's abundant blessings guiding my path. Though I am guided, I take action to clear space for my goal so I can always feel the way I want to feel.

Sagittarius Full Moon Ritual: Cultivating Self-Confidence

This ritual for the Full Moon in Sagittarius utilizes Tarot to visualize your goal and intention. Create a visual and symbolic pathway using Tarot cards that represent the stages of your journey, aligning with Sagittarius's expansive and visionary energy.

You Need:
- A Tarot deck.
- A candle in a color that resonates with your intention (white for general purposes or a color aligned with your specific goal).
- Optional: Crystals, oils, or other items that support your intention and/or goal.

To Begin:
- Choose a quiet and comfortable area where you can focus without interruptions. Arrange your space in a way that feels sacred and conducive to divination.
- Begin by reflecting on what you want to bring into your life. Visualize your goal in detail, including how it feels to achieve it.

The Ritual:
- Shuffle your Tarot deck while focusing on your intention.
- Draw a card for each phase or step you envision on your journey towards this goal. Lay the cards out in front of you in the order they need to be addressed.

- Perform your preferred method of grounding or cast a circle to create a protected and sacred space for your ritual.
- Light your chosen candle, focusing on its flame as a symbol of Sagittarius's fiery energy.
- Starting with the first card, visualize yourself successfully navigating each stage represented by the Tarot cards. Feel the emotions and experiences as if they are happening now.
- Mentally or physically, if space allows, move from one card to the next, embodying the journey towards your goal. With each step, affirm your ability to overcome challenges and progress forward.
- Once you reach the final card, take a moment to bask in the feeling of accomplishment. Affirm aloud: "Under the Sagittarius Full Moon, my path is clear, my will is strong, and my success is assured."
- Leave the cards and the candle where you can see them and connect with them for three days. If you've used crystals or oils, place them with the cards to amplify their energy.
- Close your circle or grounding practice, giving thanks to the Full Moon and the Tarot for their guidance.

This Sagittarius Full Moon ritual is a powerful way to use Tarot as a tool for manifestation. By creating a visual and symbolic journey with the cards, you align with the visionary and expansive energy of Sagittarius, setting a clear path for your aspirations to unfold.

SAGITTARIUS WANING GIBBOUS MOON
Wisdom and Gratitude

SAGITTARIUS
WANING GIBBOUS MOON
QUICKIE
For the busiest of magical bees.

Busy Witch Ritual:

Draw a long arrow on a piece of paper. Start on one side and list bits of wisdom you've gathered about your life's journey so far this cycle.

Self-Care Tip:

Engage in storytelling or writing, sharing your adventures and insights in a creative way.

Affirmation:

As the Sagittarius Waning Gibbous Moon fades, I release old beliefs with gratitude, making space for new wisdom and adventures that align with my soul's journey. I make space for more experiences that will lead me to feel the way I want to feel.

Sagittarius Waning Gibbous Moon: Fiery Gratitude Practice

Combine the yin energy of gratitude with the fiery, expansive energy of Sagittarius. Express gratitude while connecting with the energy of the sacral chakra, helping the Sagittarius expansion amplify.

You Need:
- A candle or materials for a small, safe outdoor fire.
- Pen and paper if you choose to write down your gratitude list.
- Water and fire element objects to enhance the connection with the sacral chakra and Sagittarius.

To Begin:
- Set up your space outdoors if possible, or indoors with fire or water elements. Arrange your items in a way that feels expansive and connected to possibility.
- Begin by lighting your candle or creating a small fire in a safe outdoor space. As you do so, focus on the warm, expansive energy of Sagittarius and the receiving influence of the sacral chakra.

The Ritual:
- Sit comfortably near the flame and start reflecting on all the things you are grateful for. Think about the blessings in your life, the lessons learned, and the abundance yet to come.

- If you prefer, write down your thoughts of gratitude on paper. Express everything you feel thankful for, big or small.
- Spend time visualizing each aspect of gratitude. Feel the warmth of the fire and the grounding energy, enhancing your feelings of thankfulness.
- If you've written your gratitude list, carefully place the paper into the fire. As it burns, imagine your gratitude being released into the universe, magnifying its abundance.
- Stay with the fire or candle until it burns down naturally, continuously holding a space of gratitude.
- Conclude the ritual by expressing thanks to the universe, the sacral chakra, and the Sagittarius moon for their guidance and abundance.

This Waning Gibbous Moon ritual in Sagittarius is a powerful way to blend the fiery energy of the sign with the reflective practice of gratitude. By focusing on thankfulness and expanding yourself with the sacral chakra energy, you create an energy that activates your spirit and your connection to the world around you. Embrace this ritual as a reminder of the abundance in your life and the power of gratitude to transform your perspective and attract even more blessings.

SAGITTARIUS THIRD QUARTER MOON
Let Go of Limitations

SAGITTARIUS
THIRD QUARTER MOON
QUICKIE
For the busiest of magical bees.

Busy Witch Ritual:

Identify any beliefs or habits that may have limited your freedom or growth. Consciously release these to make room for new adventures.

Self-Care Tip:

Create a decluttering session focused not just on physical space, but also on mental and emotional spaces, letting go of any constraints that hinder your expansive nature.

Affirmation:

Under the Sagittarius Third Quarter Moon, I embrace the power of transformation, letting go of what no longer serves me to journey towards my truest, most expansive self. I invite dreams and clarity for the future as I continue on my path to feel the way I want to feel.

Sagittarius Third Quarter Moon Ritual: Culinary Adventure

Embrace the sign's adventurous and optimistic spirit in the kitchen. Get creative with cooking, using intuition and spontaneity rather than strict recipes, to nourish your body as you prepare for the new lunar cycle.

You Need:
- Choose a variety of ingredients that inspire you. Opt for items you've never used before or unusual combinations that spark your curiosity.
- Have basic cooking tools and utensils ready, but be prepared to improvise.
- Play your favorite upbeat music to set a fun and adventurous mood in the kitchen.

To Begin:
- Ensure your kitchen space is clean and inviting for a creative cooking experience.
- Begin by setting your intention to be open, creative, and joyful in your culinary exploration. Embrace the Sagittarius energy of adventure and optimism.

The Ritual:

- Select ingredients that appeal to you in the moment. Trust your instincts and let your intuition guide your choices.
- Experiment with flavors and textures, combining ingredients in new and exciting ways. Remember, this is about exploration and fun, not perfection.
- As you cook, keep the Sagittarius energy in mind. Be bold and extravagant in your culinary creations. Whether it's a lavish dessert, an exotic smoothie, or a hearty stew, let your imagination run wild.
- Dance, sing, or simply enjoy the music as you cook. Let the process be as enjoyable as the outcome. Cooking is not just about the dish you create, but the joy and adventure in creating it.
- After your cooking session, take a moment to journal about the experience. Give your dish a name, describe how it turned out, and note how it tasted.
- Reflect on how this creative process felt and what it taught you about spontaneity and intuition.
- If possible, share your culinary creation with others. Sagittarius loves sharing experiences, and food is a wonderful way to connect.
- Use this ritual as a reminder to infuse joy and creativity into your daily routines, not just in cooking, but in all aspects of life.

This Third Quarter Moon ritual in Sagittarius is a delightful way to connect with the sign's adventurous spirit. By getting creative in the kitchen, you embrace a sense of freedom and joy, nourishing both your body and soul as you prepare for the new lunar cycle ahead.

SAGITTARIUS WANING CRESCENT MOON
Release and Renewal

SAGITTARIUS
WANING CRESCENT MOON
QUICKIE
For the busiest of magical bees.

Busy Witch Ritual:

Release the lunar cycle by dancing and dreaming of the next cycle.

Self-Care Tip:

Engage in a quiet, restorative activity like reading an inspiring book or practicing gentle yoga, allowing yourself to recharge and prepare for the new cycle ahead.

Affirmation:

As the Sagittarius Waning Crescent Moon fades, I trust in the journey ahead, knowing each step brings me closer to my deepest wisdom and adventurous spirit. I am excited about the journey as I pursue feeling the way I want to feel and know manifestation is inevitable.

Sagittarius Waning Crescent Moon Ritual: Release and Renewal

Release old patterns and set the stage for new beginnings. Combine the transformative fire energy of Sagittarius with the introspective nature of the Waning Crescent Moon, encouraging personal growth and optimism.

You Need:

- A Black Obsidian crystal for self-discovery and spiritual growth.
- A fire-safe vessel for burning the paper and a lighter or matches.
- Two blank sheets of paper.
- A black candle and a black pen.

To Begin:

- Choose a quiet and comfortable space where you can focus on your ritual without interruptions. Set up your materials in a way that feels sacred and intentional.
- Begin by lighting your black candle. As you do so, set your intention to release what no longer serves you and to welcome new possibilities.

The Ritual:

- On the first sheet of paper, write: "I am releasing what does not serve my highest good. I am entering this new cycle with a fresh and healed perspective of my reality." Below this, list what you wish to release.

- Place the black obsidian crystal on top of the paper to amplify your intention and focus on the candle flame, visualizing everything you wish to release leaving your energy field.
- When ready, fold the paper away from you, symbolizing the release of these energies.
- Safely light the paper using the candle flame and allow it to burn completely in the fire-safe vessel.
- On the second sheet of paper, write down everything you are grateful for at this moment and your biggest dreams for the future. Be bold and expansive in your aspirations.
- Fold this paper towards you, drawing these positive energies closer.
- Place the second paper under your pillow before you go to sleep. This symbolizes keeping your dreams and gratitude close, allowing them to influence your subconscious mind.
- Spend the night resting and reflecting on the ritual. Allow yourself to feel the release of the old and the welcoming of new possibilities.
- Extinguish the black candle safely, affirming your readiness for the new cycle. Acknowledge the transformation you've initiated and the growth that awaits.
- Give thanks to the Sagittarius energy for its guidance and the moon for its illuminating presence in your journey.
- Keep the black obsidian crystal with you or in a special place as a reminder of your commitment to personal growth and spiritual protection.

By consciously letting go of what no longer serves you and setting your sights on your grandest dreams, you align with the spirit of Sagittarius. This ritual sets the stage for personal growth and new beginnings, allowing you to enter the next lunar cycle with a fresh perspective and an open heart.

SAGITTARIUS RITUAL NOTES

SAGITTARIUS RITUAL NOTES

CAPRICORN

Capricorn, the tenth sign of the zodiac, is synonymous with discipline, ambition, and a strong sense of responsibility. Set lofty goals, pursue achievements with determination, and build a foundation of stability and respect. Capricorn energy drives you to climb the ladder of success, to structure your life with purpose, and to seek accomplishment through perseverance and hard work.

The mountain goat's relentless pursuit of goals can lead to a workaholic mentality or a rigid approach to life, making it difficult to adapt to change or to appreciate life's simpler pleasures. What starts as a disciplined approach to life's challenges can sometimes turn into an inflexible adherence to tradition or status.

Capricorn's energy teaches us the importance of setting goals and working diligently towards them, while also reminding us to maintain balance by nurturing our emotional well-being and valuing relationships. It encourages us to build not just a career or reputation, but also a life rich in experiences and connections.

Capricorn Moon Toolkit

Here are some suggested tools for your Capricorn moon ritual kit. Keep in mind that everything is optional and the only true requirement is your energy, magic, and belief!

🌙 **Sun Sign Dates: December 22 - January 19**

🌙 **Candle Color: Black**

🌙 **Oil or Essence: Vetiver (for ambition and grounding)**

🌙 **Herb: Comfrey (for endurance and practicality)**

🌙 **Spell Focus: Discipline and ambition**

🌙 **Element: Earth**　🌙 **Tarot: Pentacles**

🌙 **Crystal: Garnet**

🌙 **Mythology: Pan**

Capricorn in My Chart

Refer to your birth chart and look for Capricorn. It may be marked with this symbol: ♑

🌙 **House(s):**

🌙 **Planet(s):**

🌙 **Notes:**

Whenever the Moon is in Capricorn, it will highlight this part of your birth chart and you may notice heightened emotions in this area or shadow aspects of your life or energy coming to the surface.

CAPRICORN NEW MOON

Set Practical Goals

CAPRICORN NEW MOON
QUICKIE
For the busiest of magical bees.

Busy Witch Ritual:

Find a quiet space to focus. Light a brown or green candle, symbolizing Capricorn's earthy and grounded energy. Write down one realistic and achievable goal that aligns with your long-term vision. Visualize it with determination and commitment.

Self-Care Tip:

Engage in a grounding yoga sequence or a nature walk to connect with the earth and solidify your intention and goal.

Affirmation:

Under the New Moon in Capricorn, I set an intention and goal grounded in determination and discipline, trusting in my ability to build a stable and successful path towards my highest aspirations. I have what it takes to keep going no matter what comes my way as I journey to feel the way I want to feel.

Capricorn New Moon Ritual: Climbing the Mountain

♑

Understand and navigate your personal journey towards enlightenment and self-discovery. Using divination tools like pendulums, tarot, or oracle cards, you'll gain insights into the different stages of your journey and the lessons to be learned.

You Need:

- A pendulum, tarot deck, or oracle cards.
- A quiet and comfortable space for reflection.
- Notebook and pen for jotting down insights.

To Begin:

- Set up your space in a way that feels grounding and conducive to introspection. You might want to include symbols of Capricorn, like images of mountains or goats, to enhance the energy of the ritual.
- Begin by lighting a candle or incense to signify the start of your sacred practice. Take a few deep breaths to center yourself and connect with the energy of Capricorn.

The Ritual:

- Hold your pendulum or shuffle your tarot/oracle cards while focusing on your personal journey towards enlightenment.
- Ask the following questions, drawing a card or using the pendulum for each:

- What do I need to know about the beginning of this journey?
- What insights are important for the middle of this journey?
- What should I anticipate towards the end of this journey?
- What lesson am I meant to learn on this journey?
- How will I recognize the completion of this journey?

- Spend time contemplating the responses or the cards drawn. Consider how these insights apply to your current life path and the steps you're taking towards personal growth.
- Write down the insights and messages you received. Reflect on how they resonate with your experiences and aspirations.
- Conclude the divination part of the ritual by affirming your commitment to your journey. You might say, "I embrace the path before me, seeking wisdom and growth with each step I take."
- Thank the divination tools and the energy of Capricorn for their guidance. Extinguish the candle or incense as a symbol of closing the ritual.

This Capricorn New Moon ritual is a powerful way to connect with your inner wisdom and the guiding energy of Capricorn. By exploring the different stages of your personal journey, you gain valuable insights that can help illuminate your path to self-discovery and spiritual growth.

CAPRICORN WAXING CRESCENT MOON
Lay Foundations

CAPRICORN
WAXING CRESCENT MOON
QUICKIE
For the busiest of magical bees.

Busy Witch Ritual:

Create a morning affirmation like, "I am building my future," to state each morning and set the tone for the day.

Self-Care Tip:

Spend a few minutes in meditation, visualizing the foundations of your goals being laid, brick by brick.

Affirmation:

As the Waxing Crescent Moon in Capricorn grows, so does my resolve to take practical steps towards my goal and intention, steadily building the foundation for lasting achievement. I have the grit to move forward as I take steps to feel the way I want to feel.

Capricorn Waxing Crescent Moon Ritual: Grounding

♑

Ground your goal and intention with the wisdom of past experiences and the nurturing energy of the earth. Reflect on the lessons learned and how they can shape your path forward, using the grounding and practical energy of Capricorn to prepare for action.

You Need:
- Earth elements (dirt, rocks, sand, or salt).
- A bowl or jar to hold the earth.
- Water to mix with the earth.
- Your written intention or a symbol of it.

To Begin:
- Choose a quiet space where you can connect with the earth. If possible, perform this ritual outside under the Waxing Crescent moon.
- Begin by placing the earth element into your bowl or jar. As you touch and move the earth, focus on your intention and how it's rooted in your past experiences.

The Ritual:
- While interacting with the earth, think about the lessons from your past – both the successes and the challenges. Consider how these experiences have shaped you and what they can teach you about pursuing your current intention.

- Pour water into the bowl, mixing it with the earth. The water symbolizes intuition, flowing through and nourishing your intention. As you mix, listen to your inner voice and the insights it offers.
- Use your hands to shape the earth and water mixture. Add rocks or other elements to represent the strength and stability of your intention. If your intention requires a softer approach, adjust the texture accordingly.
- Imagine your intention taking root in the earth and being nourished by the water. Visualize it growing stronger as the moon waxes.
- Once you feel your intention is fully integrated with the earth, you can choose to keep the bowl as a symbol throughout the moon cycle or return it to nature, allowing the moonlight to shine upon it.
- Close the ritual by giving thanks to the earth and the moon for their guidance and support.
- Keep the bowl in a place where you can see it, reminding you of your intention and the growth it's undergoing.
- As the moon moves towards its first quarter phase, start planning actionable steps that align with the insights gained during this ritual.

This Waxing Crescent Moon ritual in Capricorn is a powerful way to ground your goal and intention in the wisdom of your past experiences and the nurturing energy of the earth. By physically and symbolically connecting your goals with these elements, you prepare yourself for practical and informed action in the coming phases of the moon.

CAPRICORN FIRST QUARTER MOON

Assess and Plan

CAPRICORN
FIRST QUARTER MOON
QUICKIE
For the busiest of magical bees.

Busy Witch Ritual:

Sit somewhere you don't usually sit and contemplate what action you'll take next.

Self-Care Tip:

Enjoy a brief session of deep stretching or a calming tea ritual to relax and maintain focus.

Affirmation:

With the First Quarter Moon in Capricorn, I embrace discipline and determination, confidently overcoming obstacles and steadily progressing towards my ambitions. I have what it takes to move past barriers and am excited to reach new heights.

Capricorn First Quarter Moon Ritual: Time Mastery

♑

This ritual for the First Quarter Moon in Capricorn focuses on practical action and time management. Identify and release activities that drain your time, enabling you to use your resources more efficiently to manifest your intentions.

You Need:
- A notebook or journal for list-making.
- A timer to track your activities.
- A quiet space where you can focus without distractions.

To Begin:
- Set up your space in a way that feels organized and conducive to focus. You might want to include symbols of Capricorn, like images of clocks or mountains, to enhance the energy of the ritual.
- Begin by lighting a candle or incense to signify the start of your focused practice. Take a few deep breaths to center yourself and connect with the disciplined energy of Capricorn.

The Ritual:
- In your notebook, create a list of all the activities that consume your time unnecessarily. Include tasks you do out of obligation, distractions, and anything that can be delegated.

- Be honest and thorough in your assessment.
- Use a timer to start tracking how long your daily activities actually take. This will help you gain a realistic understanding of your time usage.
- Note these times in your journal or lunar cycle tracker.
- Close your eyes and visualize yourself efficiently managing your time. Imagine completing tasks with ease and having extra time for your personal goals and doing things that leave you feeling the way you want to feel.
- Affirm aloud: "I release time-consuming distractions and reclaim my time. I am the master of my schedule, and every moment is used wisely."
- Conclude by giving thanks for the insights gained. Feel empowered by your new understanding of time management.
- Extinguish the candle or incense as a symbol of closing the ritual.
- Implement the changes you've identified. Start delegating tasks where possible and eliminate unnecessary distractions.

This First Quarter Moon ritual in Capricorn is a practical approach to harnessing the disciplined energy of the sign. By focusing on time management and releasing unproductive habits, you pave the way for efficient action towards your goals and intention, aligning with the pragmatic and goal-oriented nature of Capricorn.

CAPRICORN WAXING GIBBOUS MOON
Fine-Tune and Persevere

CAPRICORN
WAXING GIBBOUS MOON
QUICKIE
For the busiest of magical bees.

Busy Witch Ritual:

Keeping your end goal in sight, get outside and tap into the powerful wisdom of nature to fuel trust in yourself and the journey.

Self-Care Tip:

Take a warm bath with earthy herbs or incense like cedarwood or vetiver to stay grounded yet rejuvenated.

Affirmation:

As the Waxing Gibbous Moon shines in Capricorn, I trust in my resilience and wisdom, knowing that each step I take brings me closer to my highest goals. The power to feel the way I want to feel is always within me.

Capricorn Waxing Gibbous Moon Ritual: Inner Trust

♑

Strengthen your resolve and trust in your path, especially when doubts arise. It combines the grounding and ambitious energy of Capricorn with the illuminating power of the Waxing Moon to reinforce your confidence and determination.

You Need:
- A gold candle to symbolize success and confidence.
- Eight pieces of Citrine for manifestation and positivity.
- Incense or flower essences for cleansing and anointing the candle.

To Begin:
- Set up your space in a way that feels structured and conducive to concentration. You might want to include symbols of Capricorn, like images of mountains or structured geometric patterns, to enhance the energy of the ritual.
- Begin by lighting incense or anointing your candle with flower essences, if you choose to do so. Take a few deep breaths to center yourself and connect with the disciplined energy of Capricorn.

The Ritual:
- Arrange the citrine pieces in a circle, symbolizing the cycle of growth and manifestation.

- Place the gold candle in the center of the circle. As you light it, affirm: "I banish doubt and fully trust in the universe to deliver the perfect outcome. And so it is."
- Spend time journaling positive affirmations about trust, focusing on your confidence in the universe's plan. If you prefer, meditate on releasing doubt and welcoming trust.
- Visualize your goals and intention being met with success and fulfillment.
- Affirm aloud: "With the grounding energy of Capricorn and the growing light of the moon, my resolve is strong, and my path is clear."
- Allow the candle to burn down safely, symbolizing the release of doubt and the strengthening of your trust.
- Conclude the ritual by giving thanks for the clarity and confidence gained. Feel empowered by your renewed trust in your journey.
- Keep the Citrine stones in a place where you can see them, reminding you of your commitment to trust and confidence until the full moon.
- Continue to use affirmations and visualization techniques to reinforce your trust in the universe and your own abilities.

This Waxing Gibbous Moon ritual in Capricorn is a powerful way to align with the sign's ambitious and disciplined energy. By focusing on banishing doubt and reinforcing trust, you pave the way for confident action towards your goals, embodying the determined spirit of Capricorn.

CAPRICORN FULL MOON

Celebrate Achievements

CAPRICORN FULL MOON
QUICKIE
For the busiest of magical bees.

Busy Witch Ritual:

Acknowledge the milestones you've reached. Celebrate your discipline and the progress made, no matter how small. Put your hands on the earth or a plant and charge yourself with energy to keep going.

Self-Care Tip:

Journal in a peaceful environment or take a hike that allows you to look out at the world from a new perspective.

Affirmation:

Under the luminous Capricorn Full Moon, I celebrate my achievements and embrace the strength and discipline that guide me towards my greatest aspirations. I leave behind anything that does not serve my highest good and I move forward with clarity and space to feel the way I want to feel.

Capricorn Full Moon Ritual: Tarot Guidance and Intuition

♑

This ritual for the Full Moon in Capricorn uses Tarot as a tool for guidance, helping you decide whether to release or continue manifesting your intention. It combines the practical, goal-oriented energy of Capricorn with the intuitive insights offered by Tarot, enhanced by the psychic properties of Lapis Lazuli.

You Need:

- A tarot deck for guidance.
- A Lapis Lazuli stone to enhance intuition and psychic awareness.
- Notebook and pen for jotting down insights.

To Begin:

- Set up your space in a way that feels calm and conducive to hearing your inner self. You might want to include symbols of Capricorn, like images of mountains or structured patterns, to enhance the energy of the ritual.
- Begin by holding the lapis lazuli stone, connecting with its energy. Take a few deep breaths to center yourself and connect with the grounding energy of Capricorn and the illuminating power of the full moon.

The Ritual:

- Shuffle your tarot deck while focusing on your current intention or goal and the energy of the Full Moon.

- Draw a card for each of the following questions:
  - How can I best utilize this Full Moon energy?
  - What should I release?
  - What should I move forward with?
  - How can I best utilize my intuition here?
- Spend time contemplating the responses or the cards drawn. Consider how these insights apply to your current situation and the steps you're taking towards your goals.
- Write down the insights and messages you received. Reflect on how they resonate with your experiences and aspirations.
- Conclude the tarot reading by affirming your trust in your intuition and the guidance received. You might say, "I embrace the wisdom revealed by the tarot under the Capricorn Full Moon, guiding my path with clarity and purpose."
- Thank the tarot and the Lapis Lazuli for their guidance. Extinguish any candles or close your space in a way that feels respectful and complete.
- Keep the Lapis Lazuli stone with you or in a special place as a reminder of your commitment to taking actions that allow you to feel the way you want to feel.

This Full Moon ritual in Capricorn is a powerful way to connect with your inner wisdom and the guiding energy of Capricorn. By exploring the tarot's insights, you gain valuable guidance that can help illuminate your path to achieving your goals and making the most of the full moon's energy.

CAPRICORN WANING GIBBOUS MOON
Bask in Progress

CAPRICORN
WANING GIBBOUS MOON
QUICKIE
For the busiest of magical bees.

Busy Witch Ritual:

Stand with your arms to the sky and imagine you're standing at the top of a mountain. What new perspective can you consider on your progress so far?

Self-Care Tip:

Tend to the earth in some way. Ground yourself and give back at the same time.

Affirmation:

As the Capricorn Waning Gibbous Moon guides me, I embrace the wisdom of perseverance and patience, trusting that my efforts are building a foundation for lasting success and fulfillment. I give back to the collective through being myself and creating a life that feels like magic.

Capricorn Waning Gibbous Moon Ritual: Reflect on Progress

♑

Reflect on your journey towards your intention, recognize your strengths, and understand the work that remains. Combine the reflective nature of the Waning Moon with the practical and achievement-focused energy of Capricorn.

You Need:
- A Tarot deck.
- A quiet and comfortable space for contemplation.
- Notebook and pen for jotting down insights and reflections.

To Begin:
- Set up your space in a way that feels conducive to thinking, clarity, and calm. You might want to include symbols of Capricorn, such as images of mountains or earthy elements, to enhance the energy of the ritual.
- Begin by grounding yourself. Take a few deep breaths, feeling a connection to the earth and the stabilizing energy of Capricorn.

The Ritual:
- Light a candle or some incense to signify the creation of your sacred practice. As you do so, set your intention to gain clarity and wisdom from your reflections.

- Shuffle your Tarot deck while focusing on your journey throughout this moon cycle and your intention.
- Draw a card for each of the following questions:
  - How did I embody this intention at the beginning of this moon cycle?
  - What energy did I embrace in moving towards this intention?
  - What energy was I resistant to in moving towards this intention?
  - How will I embody this intention at the end of this moon cycle?
- Spend time contemplating the meaning of each card drawn. Consider how these insights apply to your journey and the progress you've made.
- Reflect on the energies you embraced and those you resisted, and how they have shaped your path towards your intention.
- Write down your thoughts and interpretations of each Tarot card. Note any revelations or surprises that came up during the reading.
- Reflect on how you can continue to embody your intention as the moon cycle comes to a close.
- Conclude the Tarot reading by affirming your commitment to your intention and your journey. You might say, "I honor the progress I've made and the lessons I've learned. I am ready to continue growing and achieving."
- Thank the Tarot for its guidance and wisdom. Extinguish the candle or incense as a symbol of closing the ritual.
- Take a few moments to sit in silence, absorbing the insights and energies of the ritual.

This ritual not only celebrates your achievements but also prepares you for the next steps in your journey, embodying the disciplined and goal-oriented spirit of Capricorn.

CAPRICORN THIRD QUARTER MOON
Reevaluate and Adjust

CAPRICORN
THIRD QUARTER MOON
QUICKIE
For the busiest of magical bees.

Busy Witch Ritual:

Take stock of what's working and what isn't. Make necessary adjustments to your plans or strategies. Be efficient and practical in your approach.

Self-Care Tip:

Engage in a structured decluttering session, be it in your physical space or digital files, to eliminate any unnecessary distractions and streamline your focus.

Affirmation:

Under the Capricorn Third Quarter Moon, I release what no longer serves my journey, making space for growth and stability, grounded in the wisdom of my experiences. I can see the path forward and have what it takes to feel the way I want to feel.

Capricorn Third Quarter Moon Ritual: Self-Reward

♑

Recognize and reward yourself for the achievements and progress you've made throughout the moon cycle. Appreciate the effort you've put into both big tasks and small daily activities, aligning with Capricorn's energy.

You Need:

- A notebook or journal.
- A pen or pencil.
- A candle or incense to create a serene atmosphere.

To Begin:

- Set up your space in a way that feels calming. Light a candle or incense to signify the start of a sacred time.
- Take a few deep breaths to center yourself and connect with the grounding energy of Capricorn.

The Ritual:

- In your notebook, start listing all the achievements and tasks you've completed during this moon cycle, no matter how small or big they seem. Include everything from personal care, work-related tasks, to acts of kindness.
- Reflect on each achievement and acknowledge the effort and dedication it took.

- At the end of your list, contemplate a suitable reward for all your hard work. Choose something that truly feels like a treat or a celebration of your efforts.
- Write down this reward, making a commitment to yourself to follow through with it.
- After listing your achievements and deciding on a reward, affirm aloud: "I acknowledge my hard work and dedication. I deserve to celebrate my progress and treat myself with kindness and appreciation."
- Close your eyes and visualize yourself enjoying the reward you've chosen. Feel the satisfaction and joy of acknowledging your efforts and treating yourself.
- Conclude the ritual by giving thanks for your abilities, efforts, and the progress you've made. Feel gratitude for the opportunity to recognize and reward yourself.
- Extinguish the candle or incense, symbolizing the end of the ritual and the beginning of your self-reward.
- Follow through with the reward you promised yourself. Whether it's a simple treat or a special activity, make sure to do it as a celebration of your hard work.
- Keep the list of achievements in a place where you can see it, reminding you of what you've accomplished during this moon cycle.

By taking the time to recognize your achievements and treat yourself, you align with Capricorn's values of responsibility, discipline, and self-respect. This ritual not only celebrates your progress but also reinforces the importance of self-care and appreciation in your journey.

CAPRICORN WANING CRESCENT MOON
Rest and Reflect

CAPRICORN
WANING CRESCENT MOON
QUICKIE
For the busiest of magical bees.

Busy Witch Ritual:

Write a list of all the hard things you made it through this lunar cycle and release everything on the list.

Self-Care Tip:

Enjoy a quiet evening with a focus on self-reflection, such as reading a thought-provoking book or journaling, to gather your thoughts and prepare for the new cycle.

Affirmation:

As the Capricorn Waning Moon fades, I embrace the power of letting go, trusting in the natural cycle of renewal and the strength of my inner resilience. I carry the ability to do hard things with me and take pride knowing I am creating a life that allows me to feel the way I want to feel.

Capricorn Waning Crescent Moon Ritual: Reflection

♑

Focus on strategic planning and reflection. Assess your progress towards your long-term goals, identifying resources and barriers, and setting intentions for the upcoming lunar cycle, aligning with Capricorn's practical and methodical approach.

You Need:
- A notebook or planner.
- A pen or pencil.
- A candle or incense for focus and clarity.

To Begin:
- Set up your space in a way that feels organized and conducive to deep thought. Light a candle or incense if you wish, to signify the start of a focused and strategic session.
- Begin by lighting the candle or incense. Take a few deep breaths to center yourself and connect with the disciplined and strategic energy of Capricorn.

The Ritual:
- On a blank piece of paper or a fresh page in your planner, write your overarching goal for the year at the top.

- Divide the paper into four columns:
    - Achievements: List all the things you have achieved towards your big goal.
    - Potential Actions: Brainstorm actions that could bring you closer to your goal.
    - Resources: Identify physical, internal, and external resources available to you.
    - Barriers: Note down external and internal barriers, including limiting beliefs.
- Reflect on each column, considering how your past actions have moved you forward and what remains to be done.
- Think about how you can utilize your resources and overcome the barriers.
- Affirm aloud: "I am equipped with the tools and wisdom to achieve my goals. Each step I take brings me closer to my aspirations."
- Conclude your planning session by giving thanks for the insights gained. Feel empowered by your strategic approach.
- Extinguish the candle or incense, symbolizing the end of the ritual and the beginning of a new phase of action.

This ritual not only helps you to stay on track with your goal and intention but also reinforces the importance of being methodical and resourceful in your approach to achieving success. Use this to plan for the year ahead and cast the vision for how you want to feel.

CAPRICORN RITUAL NOTES

CAPRICORN RITUAL NOTES

AQUARIUS

Aquarius, the eleventh sign of the zodiac, embodies innovation, individuality, and a forward-thinking approach. Aquarius energy encourages you to think outside the box, to be a visionary, and to advocate for social change and community betterment.

The water bearer's pursuit of ideals can lead to a sense of detachment or aloofness, making it challenging to form deep emotional connections or to appreciate the value of tradition and convention. The desire for progress and change can sometimes evolve into a rigid adherence to one's own beliefs, overlooking the importance of empathy and emotional understanding.

Aquarius's energy teaches us the importance of embracing our individuality and using our unique talents for the greater good. It reminds us to balance our visionary ideas with practicality and to connect with others not just on an intellectual level but also through shared human experiences. Dream of a better future while also cherishing the connections and traditions that ground us in the present.

Aquarius Moon Toolkit

Here are some suggested tools for your Aquarius moon ritual kit. Keep in mind that everything is optional and the only true requirement is your energy, magic, and belief!

🌙 **Sun Sign Dates: January 20 - February 18**

🌙 **Candle Color: Electric Blue**

🌙 **Oil or Essence: Eucalyptus (for innovation and openness)**

🌙 **Herb: Lemon Balm (for uniqueness and intellect)**

🌙 **Spell Focus: Innovation and humanitarianism**

🌙 **Element: Air**   🌙 **Tarot: Swords**

🌙 **Crystal: Aquamarine**

🌙 **Mythology: The Youthful Shepard**

Aquarius in My Chart

Refer to your birth chart and look for Aquarius. It may be marked with this symbol: ♒

🌙 **House(s):**

🌙 **Planet(s):**

🌙 **Notes:**

Whenever the Moon is in Aquarius, it will highlight this part of your birth chart and you may notice heightened emotions in this area or shadow aspects of your life or energy coming to the surface.

AQUARIUS NEW MOON

Release Resistance

AQUARIUS NEW MOON
QUICKIE
For the busiest of magical bees.

Busy Witch Ritual:

Light a blue candle, symbolizing Aquarius's airy and intellectual energy. Brainstorm ways to reach your goal and feel the way you want to feel. Visualize it with excitement and openness to new possibilities.

Self-Care Tip:

Engage in a stimulating activity like a puzzle or a brainstorming session to clear your mind and set your intention with creativity.

Affirmation:

I embrace the innovative energy of the Aquarius New Moon, opening my heart and mind to unique ideas and connections. I am a catalyst for positive change, both in my life and in my community, and I trust in the universe to guide me on this journey of growth and self-discovery. I am available for unexpected ways to feel the way I want to feel.

Aquarius New Moon Ritual: Releasing Resistance

♒

Envision your future and identify any resistance or obstacles that might be hindering your progress. Combine the innovative and forward-thinking energy of Aquarius with the introspective and initiating power of the New Moon.

You Need:
- Items that symbolize your future goals (photos, vision board, etc.).
- A notebook and pen for reflections.
- A timer or alarm.

To Begin:
- Set up your space in a way that feels open and conducive to deep thought. You might want to include items that represent your future aspirations.
- Begin by sitting comfortably in your space. Take a few deep breaths to center yourself and connect with the innovative energy of Aquarius.

The Ritual:
- Close your eyes and start envisioning your future. What does it look like? Where are you? Who are you with? What are you doing?
- Allow your imagination to roam freely, picturing your ideal future in as much detail as possible.
- Set your timer or alarm for a comfortable duration to ensure you stay focused.

- After envisioning your future, reflect on any potential obstacles or resistance that might prevent you from achieving these goals. Be honest with yourself about what's holding you back.
- Write down these resistances in your notebook. It could be material possessions, fears, limiting beliefs, or external circumstances.
- For each point of resistance you've identified, write a statement of release. For example, "I release my attachment to [obstacle] to make room for my future."
- Visualize yourself letting go of these obstacles, one by one, freeing yourself to move towards your envisioned future.
- Create an affirmation that signifies your commitment to moving forward. For instance, "I am open to change and ready to embrace new opportunities that lead me to my goals."
- Conclude your ritual by affirming your intention to the New Moon. You might say, "Under this New Moon in Aquarius, I embrace change and release resistance, moving confidently towards my future."
- Take a few deep breaths to ground yourself, then gently open your eyes.
- Keep the list of resistances and your statements of release somewhere you can see them regularly. Use them as reminders to let go of what no longer serves your higher purpose.

By envisioning your future and consciously releasing resistance, you set the stage for transformation and growth in alignment with your true aspirations. Each step forward, no matter how small, is a step towards realizing your dreams under the auspicious energy of the New Moon in Aquarius.

AQUARIUS WAXING CRESCENT MOON

Explore New Ideas

AQUARIUS
WAXING CRESCENT MOON
QUICKIE
For the busiest of magical bees.

Busy Witch Ritual:

Identify unique and unconventional steps towards your goal and intention. Incorporate these ideas into your daily routine, perhaps while commuting or during lunch breaks. An affirmation like, "I embrace new ideas to fulfill my dreams," can be powerful.

Self-Care Tip:

Spend a few minutes each day on a hobby or activity that stimulates your mind and encourages innovative thinking.

Affirmation:

As the Aquarius Waxing Crescent Moon grows, so does my courage to explore uncharted territories. I trust in my vision and embrace the journey with an open mind and a spirit of innovation. Each step I take is a step towards a future filled with exciting possibilities and newfound freedom. I believe in my ability to feel the way I want to feel and am open to innovation along the way.

Aquarius Waxing Crescent Moon Ritual: Cultivating Ideas

This ritual for the Waxing Crescent Moon in Aquarius is designed to harness the innovative and intellectual energy of Aquarius to generate ideas and take the first steps towards actualizing your intentions.

You Need:
- A quiet, comfortable space for contemplation.
- A candle (preferably in a color that resonates with Aquarius energy, like blue or silver).
- A journal and a pen for recording your ideas.

To Begin:
- Set up your space in a way that feels conducive to creativity and deep thought. Light the candle to signify the start of a focused and imaginative session.
- Take a few deep breaths to center yourself and connect with the intellectual and innovative energy of Aquarius.

The Ritual:
- Close your eyes and visualize a blank whiteboard in front of you, representing a space of infinite possibilities.
- Allow your mind to freely generate ideas on how to bring your intention to life. Imagine yourself writing words or drawing pictures on this whiteboard. Let your imagination run wild without limitations.

- When your flow of ideas begins to slow, gently open your eyes.
- Pick up your journal and start writing down the ideas you remember. Focus on what feels achievable and exciting at this moment.
- Conclude your ritual by blowing out the candle, visualizing that you are infusing your ideas with life and energy.
- Affirm aloud: "With this breath, I activate my ideas and step forward into action."
- Keep your journal handy and refer to it as you start to implement your ideas.
- Take at least one small action in the following days that aligns with the ideas you generated during the ritual.
- Use the affirmation you created whenever you need a boost of motivation or inspiration.

This Waxing Crescent Moon ritual in Aquarius aligns you with the sign's energy of innovation, intellectual stimulation, and forward-thinking. By actively engaging in a creative visualization process and committing your ideas to paper, you're taking the first steps towards bringing your intention to life. Aquarius energy encourages you to think outside the box and embrace unconventional methods, so be open to unique and creative approaches as you move forward.

AQUARIUS FIRST QUARTER MOON
Experiment and Innovate

AQUARIUS
FIRST QUARTER MOON

QUICKIE

For the busiest of magical bees.

Busy Witch Ritual:

List three things you do every day. Add one small action you can take with each to get you closer to your future vision.

Self-Care Tip:

Engage in a fun, experimental activity like trying a new recipe or DIY project to stimulate your creativity and adaptability.

Affirmation:

Under the Aquarius First Quarter Moon, I am empowered to break barriers and create change. My actions are guided by my unique insights and progressive thinking. I confidently step forward, knowing that each decision I make is a bold stride towards shaping a better world and a more authentic self. I act in accordance with how I want to feel, not necessarily with how I feel right now.

Aquarius First Quarter Moon Ritual: Innovate Your Path

〜〜

The Aquarius First Quarter Moon is a powerful time for innovation, creativity, and embracing your unique traits to manifest your intentions. This phase brings the energy of action and forward momentum. Break free from convention, think outside the box, and find new pathways to achieve your goals.

You Need:

- A notebook or journal.
- A blue or silver candle.
- Amethyst or Labradorite crystal.
- A deck of tarot or oracle cards.
- Flower essence of rosemary or eucalyptus.
- Incense for cleansing (optional).

To Begin:

- Find a quiet space where you can focus and feel at ease.
- Begin by cleansing the area with incense, clearing away any lingering energies. As you do this, set the intention for fresh, creative energy to fill the space.

The Ritual:

- Light a blue or silver candle, calling in the innovative and forward-thinking energy of Aquarius.

- Sit comfortably, close your eyes, and take a few deep breaths. Focus on your intention for this lunar cycle—what goal are you working toward? What unique qualities do you possess that could help you manifest this desire? Let your intention become clear in your mind.

- Using your tarot or oracle deck, pull a card to represent the energy or guidance you need to innovate your path forward. Reflect on the card's message and how it might offer a fresh perspective.

- In your notebook or journal, draw a winding path that represents your journey toward your goal. At the beginning of the path, write down your current state—where you are now in relation to your intention. Along the path, note different steps or milestones that can lead you to your desired outcome. Let this be a creative process—draw symbols, write words, or create doodles that represent your approaches.

- Reflect on the unique traits and qualities that make you, you. How can these be utilized to bring more creativity, innovation, or originality to your path?

- Anoint yourself and your notebook with a few drops of rosemary or eucalyptus essence to clear the mind and promote visionary thinking. Hold the Amethyst or Labradorite crystal in your hand, close your eyes, and visualize yourself confidently walking your unique path, reaching your intention with ease and creativity.

- To seal your ritual, blow out your candle and say aloud, "I walk my path with confidence, creativity, and innovation, honoring my unique gifts. So it is." Allow any remaining smoke to carry your intention into the universe.

Break free from the ordinary and explore innovative ways to reach your goals. Embrace your unique traits and think creatively to find new paths unfolding before you that you may not have considered before. Trust yourself and be bold.

AQUARIUS WAXING GIBBOUS MOON
Your Unique Purpose

AQAURIUS
WAXING GIBBOUS MOON
QUICKIE
For the busiest of magical bees.

Busy Witch Ritual:

If you've been doing something that really isn't working, release the status quo way of doing it and call in an innovative approach.

Self-Care Tip:

Relax in a warm bath with a cup of peppermint tea to stimulate your mind while soothing your body.

Affirmation:

As the Aquarius Waxing Gibbous Moon illuminates my path, I trust in the unfolding of my vision. I am open to innovative ideas and embrace the unexpected. My intuition is my guide, leading me towards a future filled with possibilities and breakthroughs. I have the unique ability to allow myself to feel the way I want to feel.

Aquarius Waxing Gibbous Moon Ritual: Your Unique Message

♒

This ritual for the Waxing Gibbous Moon in Aquarius is designed to help you connect with your inner message and trust in your unique path. Embrace what truly ignites your passion and use that energy to make a positive impact.

- Items to create a talisman (this could be a stone, a piece of jewelry, a small cloth pouch, or any item that resonates with you).
- A notebook and pen for writing your affirmation.
- Crystals or other items that symbolize clarity, communication, and self-trust (like aquamarine or clear quartz).

To Begin:
- Set up your space in a way that feels open to clarity and receiving. Place your talisman-making materials and any symbolic items in front of you.
- Begin by sitting comfortably in your space. Take a few deep breaths to center yourself and connect with the innovative and authentic energy of Aquarius.

The Ritual:
- Reflect on the questions about your life's purpose, passions, and what truly excites you. Allow your thoughts to flow freely without judgment.

411

- Write down the insights that come to you, focusing on what feels most aligned with your soul right now.
- Based on your reflections, create a talisman that represents your unique message. This could involve inscribing a stone, crafting a piece of jewelry, or preparing a small pouch with symbolic items.
- Alternatively, write a powerful affirmation that encapsulates your message and intention.
- Hold your talisman or affirmation in your hands. Visualize it being infused with the energy of the Waxing Gibbous Moon and your own conviction.
- Place it in a spot where it can absorb the moon's energy overnight.
- Repeat your affirmation aloud, feeling its power and truth. If you have a talisman, hold it close to your heart.
- Commit to taking at least one action that aligns with your message in the coming days.
- Conclude your ritual by giving thanks for the clarity and inspiration provided by the Aquarius Moon. Feel empowered to share your unique light with the world.
- Keep your talisman or affirmation in a place where you can see it daily as a reminder of your purpose and path. Release it at the end of the lunar cycle.

This Waxing Gibbous Moon ritual in Aquarius encourages you to trust in your unique path and message, embracing the qualities that make you distinct and using them to inspire and influence the world positively.

AQUARIUS FULL MOON
Celebrate Uniqueness

AQUARIUS FULL MOON
QUICKIE
For the busiest of magical bees.

Busy Witch Ritual:

Acknowledge the unique approaches you've taken. Light a candle and blow it out after letting go of the need to follow the exact right path.

Self-Care Tip:

Make a collage that celebrates your individuality and unique qualities.

Affirmation:

Under the radiant Aquarius Full Moon, I embrace my uniqueness and the power of community. I am connected to the collective wisdom, and my actions contribute to a greater good. I celebrate my individuality and the diversity around me, knowing that together, we create a harmonious and progressive world.

Aquarius Full Moon Ritual: Embrace Your Truth

≋

This ritual for the Full Moon in Aquarius is designed to help you embrace and express your inner truth. Recognize your deepest desires, unspoken thoughts, and the things holding you back, then release them to step into a more authentic version of yourself.

You Need:

- Flower essences or incense that resonate with you.
- A piece of paper and something to write with.
- A safe way to burn the paper (like a fireproof bowl) if you choose to burn it.

To Begin:

- Set up your space in a way that feels open and safe for self-expression. Drip your flower essence or light your incense to create a comforting atmosphere.
- Begin by sitting comfortably in your space. Take a few deep breaths to center yourself and connect with the liberating and authentic energy of the Aquarius Full Moon.

The Ritual:

- On the piece of paper, start by writing down five things you've never said out loud before. Be honest and unfiltered.

- Next, list ten things you would do if money wasn't a factor. Allow yourself to dream big and without limitations.
- Finally, write down three things you want to release to step into your truth and work towards your dreams.
- Fold the paper up. If possible, take it to a crossroads and bury it, symbolizing the intersection of your current path with new possibilities. If you can't do this, burning the paper at a crossroads or in a safe place works too.
- As you bury or burn the paper, visualize releasing your unspoken truths and limitations. Imagine the Full Moon's energy amplifying your intentions.
- Create an affirmation that affirms your commitment to living your truth. For example, "Under this Full Moon, I embrace my truth and step forward with authenticity and courage."
- Conclude your ritual by giving thanks to the Full Moon for its illuminating energy. Feel empowered by the act of expressing and releasing your truths.
- Take a few deep breaths to ground yourself, then gently extinguish any candles or incense.

This Full Moon ritual in Aquarius is a powerful way to harness the sign's energy of innovation, authenticity, and freedom. By speaking your truth and releasing what no longer serves you, you open the door to a life more aligned with your true self.

AQUARIUS WANING GIBBOUS MOON
Be in Gratitude

AQUARIUS
WANING GIBBOUS MOON
QUICKIE
For the busiest of magical bees.

Busy Witch Ritual:

Do something that fills your cup so you have more energy for the people in your life.

Self-Care Tip:

Gather with like-minded people in person or online to relax and mingle.

Affirmation:

As the Aquarius Waning Gibbous Moon illuminates the sky, I release any barriers to innovation and progress. I trust in the flow of change, knowing that each step back is a path forward. My mind is open, my heart is ready, and I am prepared to embrace the transformative journey ahead. I am authentically myself and am excited for what's ahead.

Aquarius Waning Gibbous Moon Ritual: Expand Gratitude

≈

Focus on practicing gratitude, particularly for the blessings in the lives of others. Move beyond self-centeredness and embrace a more communal and empathetic perspective.

You Need:
- A pen and paper for writing your gratitude list.
- A candle or matches for burning the paper.
- Incense to represent air.

To Begin:
- Set up your space in a way that feels open and connected to others. Light the candle and prepare your incense, allowing its scent to fill the area and create an atmosphere conducive to reflection and gratitude.
- Take a few deep breaths to center yourself and connect with the communal and altruistic energy of Aquarius.

The Ritual:
- On the paper, write a list of people in your life for whom you are grateful. Focus on their achievements, happiness, or good fortune.
- For each person, detail what specifically you are grateful for. This could be anything from their personal successes to the joy they bring.

- Once your list is complete, gently pass the paper through the smoke of the incense. As you do this, visualize your gratitude expanding and encompassing these individuals.
- Reflect on the feeling of joy and contentment that comes from celebrating others' happiness.
- Safely burn the paper with your gratitude list. As it burns, imagine sending your positive thoughts and grateful energy out into the universe.
- As the paper turns to ash, envision any feelings of jealousy or resentment being transformed into appreciation and empathy.
- Create an affirmation that matches your commitment to embracing others' successes with gratitude. For example, "I celebrate the joy and achievements of those around me, and I am grateful for the richness they bring to my life."
- Conclude your ritual by giving thanks for the ability to feel and express gratitude for others. Feel the warmth of this expansive emotion in your heart.
- Extinguish the candle and incense, grounding yourself back in the present moment.
- Whenever feelings of jealousy or resentment arise, recall this ritual and replace those feelings with gratitude and empathy.

By focusing on the joy and success of others, you not only enrich your own emotional well-being but also contribute to a more harmonious and empathetic world. Every act of gratitude is a step towards a more connected and compassionate existence.

AQUARIUS THIRD QUARTER MOON
Detach and Reevaluate

AQUARIUS
THIRD QUARTER MOON
QUICKIE
For the busiest of magical bees.

Busy Witch Ritual:

Identify what aspects of your approach to feeling the way you want to feel haven't served your higher purpose. Detach emotionally and intellectually to gain a clearer perspective through journaling or movement.

Self-Care Tip:

Declutter your digital or mental space to create room for fresh ideas and new energy. This could involve organizing your digital files, unsubscribing from unneeded email lists, or simply spending time in quiet reflection.

Affirmation:

Under the Aquarius Third Quarter Moon, I embrace the power of detachment and objectivity. I let go of what no longer serves my highest good, making room for fresh perspectives and unique insights. I am a visionary, ready to rebuild and innovate for a brighter future.

Aquarius Third Quarter Moon Ritual: Self-Care and Dreaming

This ritual for the Third Quarter Moon in Aquarius is designed to encourage self-care and future visioning. Take time for yourself, understand your current emotional state, and indulge in activities that align you to your future.

You Need:
- A notebook or journal and a pen.
- Items that contribute to relaxation and happiness (like a favorite book, music, bath salts, a cozy blanket, etc.).

To Begin:
- Arrange your space in a way that feels soothing and personal to you. This might involve setting up a cozy corner with pillows and blankets, preparing a warm bath, or creating a calming atmosphere with soft lighting and music.
- Begin by sitting comfortably in your space. Take a few deep breaths to center yourself and connect with the introspective and independent energy of Aquarius.

The Ritual:
- In your journal, write down any feelings, emotions, or thoughts you feel the need to release. Be honest and allow yourself to express whatever comes up.

- Reflect on what activities or experiences make you feel relaxed and happy. Write these down as well.
- Choose one or more activities from your list that you can realistically do in the next three days during this moon phase.
- Schedule a specific time for this self-care activity. Write it in your calendar and inform others, if necessary, that you will be taking this time for yourself.
- Imagine your future self doing the chosen activity or activities.
- Create an affirmation that reinforces the importance of self-care and personal space. For example, "I honor my need for solitude and self-care, understanding that it replenishes my spirit and enhances my connection to myself."
- Conclude your ritual by acknowledging the time you've dedicated to yourself. Feel gratitude for the opportunity to focus on your well-being.
- Gently transition back to your regular activities, carrying with you the peace and contentment from your self-care experience.
- Reflect on how taking time for yourself impacts your mood, energy levels, and interactions with others, knowing your future self will thank you.
- Continue to use your affirmation as a reminder of the value of self-care and personal space.

This Third Quarter Moon ritual in Aquarius is a reminder of the importance of self-care and the benefits of taking time to focus on your personal needs and happiness. By honoring your need for fun and relaxation, you nurture your inner self and enhance your overall well-being, and cast a beautiful energy for future you.

AQUARIUS WANING CRESCENT MOON
Introspect and Innovate

AQUARIUS
WANING CRESCENT MOON

QUICKIE

For the busiest of magical bees.

Busy Witch Ritual:

Start ideating on what new, creative approaches you want to try in the next cycle.

Self-Care Tip:

Engage in a quiet, contemplative activity like stargazing or writing in a journal. Allow yourself the space to dream and plan for future ideas.

Affirmation:

As the Aquarius Waning Crescent Moon wanes, I trust in the flow of universal wisdom. I release my need for control, embracing the unknown with open arms. I am guided by my intuition and the collective consciousness, ready for renewal and transformation. I rest knowing my goal and intention are always working to come to me.

Aquarius Waning Crescent Moon Ritual: Release Limiting Beliefs

Focus on reflection and the release of limiting thoughts and stories that hinder your alignment with your authentic self. Embrace the Aquarian energy of liberation and transformation to clear the way for new beginnings.

You Need:

- A small saucer or plate.
- A powdery substance for drawing (like flour, sugar, or cornstarch).
- Incense for energetic cleansing.
- Crystals or herbs that aid in releasing negative energy (e.g., Smoky Quartz, rosemary).
- Access to water for rinsing.

To Begin:

- Set up your space in a way that feels cleansing and open. Place your materials neatly on a table or altar.
- Begin by grounding yourself. Take deep breaths, connecting with the innovative and transformative energy of Aquarius.

The Ritual:

- Spread the powdery substance on the plate. Reflect on the limiting beliefs or stories you've been telling yourself.

- Gently draw a word or phrase in the powder that represents these limiting beliefs.
- Light your incense, allowing the smoke to envelop the plate. As the smoke swirls around, visualize it absorbing your negative thoughts and stories.
- Focus on the feeling of release, imagining these limitations being cleansed from your spirit.
- Carefully remove any crystals or herbs from the plate.
- Take the plate to the sink. As you rinse it with water, imagine yourself as the Aquarian water bearer, washing away these old patterns and beliefs.
- Visualize the water carrying away these limitations, leaving you refreshed and open to new possibilities.
- Create an affirmation that reinforces your commitment to embracing your true self and new beginnings. For example, "I release what no longer serves me and open myself to new paths of authenticity and growth."
- Conclude your ritual by giving thanks for the opportunity to shed old patterns and embrace a fresh start.
- Feel a sense of lightness and readiness for the new lunar cycle ahead.

This Waning Crescent Moon ritual in Aquarius helps you to consciously let go of old narratives and self-imposed limitations, paving the way for a renewed sense of self as you approach the new lunar cycle. By embracing the Aquarian spirit of innovation and transformation, you open yourself to a future where you are more aligned with your true essence and potential.

AQUARIUS RITUAL NOTES

AQUARIUS RITUAL NOTES

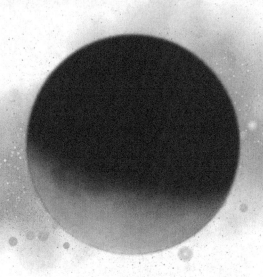

PISCES

Pisces, the twelfth and final sign of the zodiac, embodies depth, empathy, and a boundless imagination. Pisces energy encourages you to explore your inner world, to express compassion, and to engage with life through a lens of intuition and artistic creativity.

The dreamy and empathetic nature of Pisces can lead to escapism or a lack of boundaries, making it challenging to confront reality or to maintain a sense of individual identity amidst the feelings of others. Pisces energy can also lead to feelings of being overwhelmed by emotions or a tendency to lose oneself in fantasy.

Pisces's energy teaches us the importance of balance between embracing our emotional depth and maintaining a connection to the external world. It reminds us to ground our dreams and intuitions in reality and to use our imaginative and empathetic qualities to enhance our understanding of ourselves and others. Dream big and feel deeply, while also finding ways to bring those dreams into tangible form and to protect our own emotional well-being in the process.

423

Pisces Moon Toolkit

Here are some suggested tools for your Pisces moon ritual kit. Keep in mind that everything is optional and the only true requirement is your energy, magic, and belief!

🌙 Sun Sign Dates: February 19 - March 20

🌙 Candle Color: Sea Green

🌙 Oil or Essence: Sandalwood (for sensitivity and intuition)

🌙 Herb: Seaweed (for fluidity and empathy)

🌙 Spell Focus: Creativity and empathy

🌙 Element: Water   🌙 Tarot: Cups

🌙 Crystal: Amethyst

🌙 Mythology: Aphrodite and Eros

Pisces in My Chart

Refer to your birth chart and look for Pisces. It may be marked with this symbol: ♓

🌙 **House(s):**

🌙 **Planet(s):**

🌙 **Notes:**

Whenever the Moon is in Pisces, it will highlight this part of your birth chart. You may notice heightened emotions in this area or shadow aspects of your life or energy coming to the surface.

PISCES
NEW MOON
Embrace Your Intuition

PISCES NEW MOON
QUICKIE
For the busiest of magical bees.

Busy Witch Ritual:

Find a tranquil space, preferably near water. Light a candle in a soothing color like seafoam green or soft blue, symbolizing Pisces's gentle, intuitive energy. Write down an intention that aligns with your deepest intuitive insights.

Self-Care Tip:

Enjoy a meditative session near water or a relaxing bath to connect deeply with your inner wisdom.

Affirmation:

Under the Pisces New Moon, I embrace my deepest dreams and intuition. I am connected to the vast ocean of my inner wisdom, and I trust in the universe to guide my path. With compassion and creativity, I set a goal and intention that align with my soul's purpose. I am one with all that is and have what it takes to feel the way I want to feel.

Pisces New Moon Ritual: Creative Mastery

Harness the imaginative and perfectionist energies of Pisces to refine and elevate a creative skill. Combining the emotional act of creating with intuition and future visioning, you'll set a powerful intention.

You Need:

- A symbol of your chosen craft (e.g., a piece of fabric for sewing, a brush for painting).
- A blue or sea-green candle.
- A small bowl of water.
- A notebook and pen.
- Soft, inspiring music (optional).

To Begin:

- Find a quiet, comfortable area where you can focus without interruption. If possible, arrange your space near water or a representation of it.

The Ritual:

- Light the blue or sea-green candle, setting the intention to open your mind to the creative and meticulous energies of Pisces.
- Place the symbol of your craft in front of the candle. This object will serve as a physical representation of the skill you wish to perfect.

- In your notebook, write down the specific aspect of your craft you want to master during this lunar cycle. Be as detailed as possible. For example, "I intend to master the art of creating seamless buttonholes in my sewing projects."
- Dip your fingers in the bowl of water and lightly sprinkle some drops on the symbol of your craft. This act symbolizes the infusion of Piscean fluidity and adaptability into your work.
- Close your eyes and visualize yourself engaging in your craft, focusing on the perfection of the specific skill. Imagine the satisfaction and pride you will feel upon mastering this aspect.
- Repeat a positive affirmation aligned with your intention, such as, "With each stitch, I weave perfection and creativity, guided by the intuitive and meticulous energy of Pisces."
- Spend a few minutes in quiet contemplation or meditation, allowing the candle to burn (safely). Reflect on your intention and the journey you are about to embark upon.
- Extinguish the candle, thanking the Piscean energy for its guidance. Keep the notebook and craft symbol in a special place where you can see them regularly as a reminder of your intention.
- At the end of the lunar cycle, review your progress. Celebrate your achievements, no matter how small, and acknowledge the effort you've put into perfecting your craft.

This ritual is designed to align your creative energies with the intuitive and perfectionist qualities of Pisces, helping you to focus and refine your artistic abilities. Enjoy the process of honing your craft under the mystical Pisces New Moon.

PISCES WAXING CRESCENT MOON

Nurture Your Dreams

PISCES
WAXING CRESCENT MOON
QUICKIE
For the busiest of magical bees.

Busy Witch Ritual:

Set an intention to receive a message of affirmation today to confirm you are on the right track.

Self-Care Tip:

Listen to calming music or engage in a creative activity like painting to foster your dreamy Piscean nature.

Affirmation:

As the Waxing Crescent Moon glows in Pisces, I nurture my intentions with gentle care and deep understanding. My dreams are seeds, sprouting in the fertile ground of my imagination, watered by my faith and intuition. I am open to the endless possibilities that unfold before me. I easily dream of feeling the way I want to feel and am supported by all that is.

Pisces Waxing Crescent Moon Ritual: Embrace the Flow

$\mathcal{H}$

Immerse yourself in the fluid, creative energy of Pisces, enhancing your connection with your intention and the natural flow of life utilizing a bath ritual.

You Need:
- Bathtub filled with warm water.
- 5 candles in colors that resonate with you (white, blue, and purple are suggested).
- Calming water-themed music or sounds.
- Water-associated crystals (e.g., Aquamarine, Amethyst, Clear Quartz).
- Pearl or abalone shell (for external placement).

To Begin:
- Begin by filling your bathtub with warm water, adjusting the temperature to your comfort. Place your chosen crystals around the tub or carefully inside the water (except for pearl).

The Ritual:
- Start playing your selected calming, water-themed music or sounds to create a serene atmosphere.
- Position your candles safely around the bathtub.
- As you light each candle, recite the following mantras, one for each candle:

- "I am magical."
- "I am powerful."
- "I am energetically one with water."
- "My heart is filled with belief in possibilities."
- "My dreams are my realities."

- Gently ease yourself into the bathtub, feeling the comforting embrace of the water. Allow the ebbs and flows to surround you, symbolizing the fluid nature of Pisces.

- Close your eyes and focus on your breathing. With each breath, visualize your intention as already fulfilled. Imagine living in the reality where your dreams have materialized.

- Repeat the mantras again while in the water, letting each affirmation resonate with your being. Feel the words as truths, affirming your connection to your dreams and the creative power of Pisces.

- Remain in the bath, allowing yourself to be fully present in the moment. Let the water's gentle movement and the candlelight guide your thoughts, encouraging a state of peaceful meditation.

- When you feel ready, slowly rise from the bath, expressing gratitude for this moment of connection and introspection. Extinguish the candles safely, acknowledging the light they provided.

- After drying off, take a moment to journal any insights, feelings, or visions that came to you during the ritual. Reflect on how the energy of Pisces can continue to support your intention.

This ritual is designed to deepen your connection with the intuitive and imaginative energies of Pisces, helping you to align more closely with your intentions and the natural rhythms of the universe. Embrace the fluidity and creativity of Pisces as you move forward on your journey.

PISCES FIRST QUARTER MOON
Flow with Mysticism

PISCES
FIRST QUARTER MOON
QUICKIE
For the busiest of magical bees.

Busy Witch Ritual:

Close your eyes and imagine yourself swimming through the universe. Allow yourself to receive a message.

Self-Care Tip:

Participate in a gentle yoga session or take a walk by the water to connect with your emotional core and release any pent-up feelings.

Affirmation:

In the growing light of the Pisces First Quarter Moon, I embrace the courage to navigate my path with intuition and grace. Each step I take is guided by my inner wisdom, leading me closer to my true purpose. I trust in the journey, knowing my dreams are within reach. I take action to feel the way I want to feel, always supported by all that is.

Pisces First Quarter Moon Ritual: Awaken the Mystic

Harness the intuitive and imaginative energies of Pisces for taking guided action towards your intention and goal. Awaken the mystic within you and move forward with connection and confidence.

You Need:
- Your written goal and intention and possible action steps.
- Tools for connecting with your inner mystic (e.g., music, divination tools, crystals, incense, candles).
- A journal and pen for reflection.

To Begin:
- Create a serene environment that resonates with Pisces energy. This could involve dimming the lights, lighting candles, setting up crystals, or anything that helps you connect with your inner mystic.

The Ritual:
- Begin by engaging with your chosen tools. If it's music, play something that moves you deeply. If it's divination, prepare your tarot cards or pendulum. Let these tools serve as a bridge to your intuition.

- Allow yourself to be fully immersed in the experience. Let the music, the flicker of candlelight, or the energy of the crystals envelop you. Feel yourself drifting into a state where your conscious mind takes a back seat, and your intuition comes to the forefront.
- Holding your written goal, intention, and action steps in your hands, close your eyes and take deep breaths. Let the Pisces energy flow through you, awakening your inner mystic. Ask your intuition to guide you on which action steps to prioritize.
- As you feel the guidance from within, open your eyes and intuitively select the action steps that resonate most strongly with you. Trust that these are the steps your soul is guiding you towards.
- After the ritual, spend some time journaling about the experience. Write down any insights, feelings, or intuitive nudges you received. Reflect on how this process felt and how it differed from your usual decision-making process.
- Begin to implement the chosen action steps in your daily life. Remember the feeling of connection with your inner mystic and allow it to guide you as you move forward.
- Thank your inner mystic and the Pisces energy for their guidance. Extinguish any candles or incense, and close your sacred space.

This ritual is designed to deepen your connection with your intuition and the imaginative, dreamy energy of Pisces. By allowing your inner mystic to guide your actions, you align more closely with your true path, goal, and intention.

PISCES WAXING GIBBOUS MOON
Reflect and Adjust

PISCES
WAXING GIBBOUS MOON
QUICKIE
For the busiest of magical bees.

Busy Witch Ritual:

Dress in blues and yellows to align with the phase and energy of the lunar cycle.

Self-Care Tip:

Enjoy tea or fruit water and listen to the sound of ocean waves or other nature sounds that you love.

Affirmation:

As the Pisces Waxing Gibbous Moon illuminates my path, I trust in the unfolding of my destiny. My intuition is my compass, guiding me towards fulfillment. I am open to the wisdom of the universe, receiving insights and inspiration with an open heart. I have the power to feel the way I want to feel.

Pisces Waxing Gibbous Moon Ritual: Trust Potion

♓

Harness the intuitive and emotional energy of Pisces and create a potion that enhances trust in oneself, the universe, and others.

You Need:
- Blue crystal(s) (Angelite recommended), Clear Quartz crystal(s).
- Dried rose petals (suitable for tea).
- Fresh or frozen Blueberries.
- A small pot and water.
- A strainer.
- A drinking glass.

To Begin:
- Begin by creating a peaceful environment. You might want to light a candle or play soft, soothing music to align with the watery, calming energy of Pisces.

The Ritual:
- Fill your pot with water and bring it to a low boil. Add a small handful of blueberries to the water. As the water starts to boil and the blueberries begin to release their color, feel the energy of trust starting to brew.

- Turn off the heat and gently add the dried rose petals to the pot. Allow the mixture to steep, infusing the water with the essence of trust and emotional openness.
- As the potion steeps, stir it clockwise three times. With each stir, recite your affirmation about trust. This could be something like, "With each sip, my trust deepens, in myself, the universe, and those around me."
- Pour the potion through a strainer into your drinking glass. Arrange the Blue and Clear quartz crystals around the glass. These crystals will amplify the potion's energy and intention.
- Wave your dominant hand clockwise over the potion three times, reinforcing the affirmation of trust. Visualize a blue light emanating from your hand, infusing the potion with trust and intuition.
- Allow the potion to sit for nine minutes, absorbing the energies of the crystals and your intentions.
- As you drink the potion, visualize it filling you with a deep sense of trust. Imagine this energy flowing through your body, strengthening your trust in yourself, the universe, and your relationships.
- Once you have finished your potion, take a moment to feel the effects. Thank the energies of Pisces, the moon, and the crystals for their assistance. Clean up your space and return the remnants of your tea to the earth.

This ritual is designed to deepen your sense of trust and intuition, aligning with the empathetic and mystical energies of Pisces. The power of the potion is not just in the ingredients, but in the intention and energies you infuse it with.

PISCES
FULL MOON
Celebrate Emotional Growth

PISCES FULL MOON
QUICKIE
For the busiest of magical bees.

Busy Witch Ritual:

Visualize the ocean and your future dreams swimming in it. Allow the salt water to wash away anything keeping you from moving forward.

Self-Care Tip:

Take an Epsom salt bath or foot bath, or a swim in salt water if that is available to you.

Affirmation:

Under the radiant Pisces Full Moon, I embrace my deepest emotions and dreams. I am connected to the vast ocean of universal wisdom, and I allow my true self to shine brightly. My heart is open, and I am aligned with the flow of abundance and love. I am more connected than ever to how I want to feel under the Pisces Full Moon.

Pisces Full Moon Ritual: Cinnamon-Between

To harness the intuitive and transitional energies of the Pisces Full Moon, use cinnamon to enhance inner knowing and embrace the liminal space of change.

You Need:
- A cinnamon stick.
- An organza bag (optional).
- A windowsill or doorway (as an in-between space).
- Your choice of magical tools (tarot cards, crystals, etc.).

To Begin:
- Begin by finding a peaceful spot in your home where you feel most connected to the energies of the moon and Pisces. This could be a place where you usually meditate, practice yoga, or perform other rituals.

The Ritual:
- Take your cinnamon stick and place it on a windowsill, symbolizing the bridge between the inner and outer worlds. Alternatively, if you prefer, place the cinnamon stick in an organza bag and hang it in a doorway, representing the threshold between different states of being.

- As you place the cinnamon, set your intention for the moment. You might say something like, "As I place this cinnamon, may it enhance my intuition and guide me through the transitions of life, just as the moon transitions through its phases."
- Do your typical Full Moon ritual, or if you're feeling adventurous, use this time to explore new magical practices. You might want to do a tarot reading, meditate with crystals that resonate with Pisces energy, or simply sit in quiet contemplation under the moonlight.
- During your ritual, focus on the concept of liminality – the in-between spaces where transformation occurs. Allow the energy of the Pisces Full Moon to guide you into a deeper understanding of the transitions in your life and the intuition that flows through these moments.
- Reflect on how the cinnamon, known for its intuitive properties, can enhance your perception and understanding of these transitions. Visualize the cinnamon stick as a conduit for heightened intuition and clarity.
- Once your ritual is complete, thank the moon and the energy of Pisces for their guidance. If you used any additional tools, cleanse and store them appropriately.
- Leave the cinnamon stick in its place for as long as you feel necessary. It will continue to serve as a reminder of the intuitive insights and transitional energies you've embraced during this Full Moon.
- After the ritual, you might want to journal about your experiences, insights, and any intuitive messages you received. This can help solidify the energies and understandings gained during the ritual.

This experience is designed to deepen your connection with your intuition and help you navigate through life's transitions with the guidance of the Pisces Full Moon. The power of this ritual lies in your intention and openness to the energies at play.

PISCES WANING GIBBOUS MOON
Dreamy Decluttering

PISCES
WANING GIBBOUS MOON
QUICKIE
For the busiest of magical bees.

Busy Witch Ritual:

Take a bath or shower and visualize anything preventing you from dreaming big washing away.

Self-Care Tip:

Go to an art exhibit, museum, or other place that allows you to immerse yourself in the collective.

Affirmation:

As the Pisces Waning Gibbous Moon illuminates the night, I release what no longer serves my soul's journey. I trust in the natural flow of life, letting go with grace and embracing the wisdom gained. My spirit is calm, and my path is clear. I trust in my dream for my life.

Pisces Waning Gibbous Moon Ritual: Divine Decluttering

$\mathcal{H}$

To embrace the energy of the Disseminating Moon in Pisces for gratitude and decluttering, both physically and emotionally, create space for new growth and blessings.

You Need:

- Items for decluttering (unneeded objects, clothes, etc.).
- An altar broom, regular broom, or feather duster.
- A container or bag for discarded items.
- Incense for energetic space cleansing.

To Begin:

- Begin by choosing a space in your home that feels cluttered or stagnant. This could be a specific room, a closet, or even a drawer. Gather the items you need for decluttering and your broom or feather duster.
- Before you start decluttering, take a moment to ground yourself. Close your eyes and take deep breaths, connecting with the energy of the Pisces Moon. Set your intention for this ritual – to release what no longer serves you and to express gratitude for the lessons and benefits these items have provided.

The Ritual:

- Start sorting through the items in your chosen space. As you pick each item, ask yourself if it still serves a purpose in your life. If it doesn't, thank it for its service and place it in the container or bag for donation or disposal.
- Once you have decluttered the physical items, use your broom or feather duster to sweep the area. As you sweep, visualize sweeping away any stagnant energy, making room for fresh, positive energy to flow in. If you have incense, light it and use the smoke to further cleanse the space.
- As you finish cleaning the space, express your gratitude for the clarity and lightness that comes with decluttering. Acknowledge the emotional and spiritual release that accompanies the physical act of letting go. If you've used incense, allow the smoke to carry away any lingering attachments or energies.
- Once the decluttering and cleansing are complete, take a few moments to sit quietly in the newly cleared space. Reflect on the feelings of openness and potential that now fill the area. Close your ritual by expressing gratitude to the Pisces Moon for its guidance and support in this process of renewal.
- Responsibly dispose of or donate the items you've decided to let go of. As you do so, maintain the mindset of release and gratitude, knowing that these items may serve a better purpose elsewhere.

This ritual harnesses the water energy of the Pisces Moon, aiding in the release of the old and making way for new beginnings and opportunities. Decluttering is an ongoing process, and you can revisit this ritual whenever you feel the need to clear space and refresh your environment.

PISCES THIRD QUARTER MOON
Release and Let Go

PISCES
THIRD QUARTER MOON
QUICKIE
For the busiest of magical bees.

Busy Witch Ritual:

Identify emotional baggage that hasn't served you in this cycle. Consciously let go of these elements.

Self-Care Tip:

Perform a simple ritual by the water, releasing natural items to symbolize letting go, or writing to let go of old energies.

Affirmation:

I embrace the wisdom of release and transformation. As the Pisces Third Quarter Moon guides me, I let go of what no longer serves me, making space for new growth and deeper understanding. I trust in the flow of life and my intuitive power to navigate it.

Pisces Third Quarter Moon Ritual: Cleanse and Listen

♓

Use the cleansing properties of lemon water to clarify your mind and body, creating a sacred space for contemplation and self-discovery. The gentle, dreamy qualities of Pisces will guide you as you explore your deepest desires and envision your most perfect day.

You Need:
- Fresh lemons.
- A glass for the lemon water.
- A candle or incense (optional) - scents like lavender or jasmine are recommended.
- A lighter or matches for the candle/incense.
- A comfortable seat or cushion.
- A journal and pen (optional).

To Begin:
- Begin by finding a quiet and comfortable space where you won't be disturbed. This space should feel safe and peaceful, allowing you to fully immerse yourself in the ritual.

The Ritual:
- Prepare a glass of lemon water. Lemon is known for its cleansing properties, both physically and energetically. As you add the lemon to the water, set the intention for clarity and clearing.

461

- You may choose to light a candle or incense to create a calming atmosphere. Select scents that resonate with Pisces energy, such as lavender or jasmine, to enhance your connection to the water sign's intuitive and dreamy qualities.
- Sit comfortably with your glass of lemon water. Take a few deep breaths to center yourself. As you inhale, imagine drawing in peace and clarity; as you exhale, release any tension or stress.
- Holding the glass, gently ponder the questions:
  - What does your most perfect day feel like? Visualize this day in as much detail as possible. Immerse yourself in the sensations, emotions, and experiences of this ideal day.
  - How do you feel when you give to yourself? Reflect on the emotions and sensations that arise when you prioritize your well-being and self-care.
  - How do you WANT to feel when you give to yourself? Envision the ideal state of being you wish to achieve through self-love.
- Slowly sip the lemon water. With each sip, imagine absorbing the qualities of your perfect day and the feelings associated with self-giving. Let the lemon water symbolize the infusion of these positive energies into your being.
- Take some time after the meditation to journal about your experience. Write down insights, emotions, and any revelations that came to you during the ritual.
- Once you have finished your lemon water and any journaling, take a moment to thank yourself for this act of self-care. Extinguish the candle or incense if you used them. Carry the sense of renewal and energy with you as you move forward.

This ritual is designed to align with the introspective and healing energy of the Third Quarter Moon in Pisces, helping you to reconnect with your inner desires and practice self-love in a meaningful way.

PISCES WANING CRESCENT MOON
Rest and Dream

PISCES
WANING CRESCENT MOON
QUICKIE
For the busiest of magical bees.

Busy Witch Ritual:

Slow down and indulge in your dream world. Reflect on the cycle and how it has impacted your emotional and spiritual life.

Self-Care Tip:

Enjoy a quiet evening with soothing music or a gentle meditation session to wind down and embrace your dreams.

Affirmation:

I embrace the gentle flow of release under the Pisces Waning Crescent Moon. As I let go of what no longer serves me, I trust in the universe's guidance and open my heart to spiritual renewal and deeper understanding. I swim in a sea of possibility knowing there are infinite ways to feel the way I want to feel.

Pisces Waning Crescent Moon Ritual: Create a Vision Board

Creating a vision board during the Waning Crescent Moon in Pisces is a deeply intuitive and imaginative process that aligns with the introspective and dreamy qualities of Pisces. This sets the scene for the following lunar cycle.

You Need:
- Collect magazines, printed images from online sources, drawing materials, and any other creative supplies you'd like. Include felt-tip pens, paper, a large piece of cardboard or paper, glue, and scissors.

To Begin:
- Set up a peaceful space. You might want to light a candle or play some soft, inspiring music to set the mood.

The Ritual:
- Begin by flipping through your magazines or browsing your collected images. Let your intuition guide you. Choose images, words, and colors that resonate with you on a deeper level, without overthinking your choices.

- Start arranging the images and words on your cardboard or paper. There's no right or wrong way to do this — trust your instincts and let your creativity flow. You can overlap images, create collages, or organize them in any way that feels right.
- Once you're satisfied with your layout, start gluing or taping everything down. As you do this, imbue your vision board with your intentions and dreams.
- Take a step back and look at your completed vision board. Reflect on the themes, patterns, and feelings it evokes. Consider how it aligns with your current life and what changes or aspirations it reflects. Use your journal to write down your thoughts, feelings, and insights.
- Use the insights gained from your vision board to help set your intention for the upcoming lunar cycle. What areas of your life do you wish to focus on or manifest changes in?
- Place your vision board somewhere you can see it daily. Let it be a constant reminder and inspiration for your intentions and dreams.
- Your vision board is a dynamic and personal tool. It's a visual representation of your innermost desires and a map towards your future aspirations. As the moon wanes and transitions into a new cycle, your vision board will serve as a guide, helping you align your actions and thoughts with your intentions.
- Once you feel complete with your vision board and journaling, take a few moments to close your ritual. You might want to express gratitude for the insights received or simply sit in quiet contemplation, absorbing the energy of your creation.

This ritual harnesses the imaginative power of Pisces and the reflective energy of the Waning Crescent Moon, creating a perfect synergy for setting intentions and visualizing your path forward.

PISCES RITUAL NOTES

PISCES RITUAL NOTES

Made in the USA
Columbia, SC
05 December 2024

48226277R00259